nothing gold can stay

nothing gold can stay

The Colors of Grief

Mark Belletini

Skinner House Books
Boston

www.skinnerhouse.org

Printed in the United States

Cover design by Kathryn Sky-Peck
Text design by Suzanne Morgan

print ISBN: 978-1-55896-747-2
eBook ISBN: 978-1-55896-748-9

6 5 4 3 2
17 16 15

Library of Congress Cataloging-in-Publication Data

Belletini, Mark.
  Nothing gold can stay : the colors of grief / Mark Belletini.
    pages cm
  ISBN 978-1-55896-747-2 (pbk. : alk. paper)—ISBN 978-1-55896-748-9
(ebook) 1. Grief—Religious aspects—Unitarian Universalist Association—Meditations. I. Title.
  BV4909.B465 2015
  248.8'66—dc23
                              2014028819

We gratefully acknowledge permission to reprint the following:

"Celestial Music" from *Ararat* by Louise Glück, copyright © 1990 by Louise Glück, reprinted by permission of HarperCollins Publishers; "Celestial Music" from *Ararat* by Louise Glück, copyright © 1990 by Louise Glück, reprinted by permission of Carcanet Press Limited; "Nothing Gold Can Stay," from the book *The Poetry of Robert Frost* edited by Edward Connery Lathem, copyright © 1923, 1969 by Henry Holt and Company, copyright © 1951 by Robert Frost, reprinted by permission of Henry Holt and Company, LLC, all rights reserved; "Redemption Song" by Kevin Young © 2010 by Kevin Young, from *The Art of Losing: Poems of Grief and Healing*, edited by Kevin Young, reprinted by permission of Bloomsbury Publishing Inc.; "The Cure" by Albert Huffstickler © 1988 by Albert Huffstickler, reprinted by permission of Elizabeth Fraser.

To my son, Tony

contents

prelude

Nothing Gold Can Stay

Nature's first green is gold,
Her hardest hue to hold.
Her early leaf's a flower;
But only so an hour.
Then leaf subsides to leaf.
So Eden sank to grief,
So dawn goes down to day.
Nothing gold can stay.

—Robert Frost

opening words

I am a griever. I am also a father, a brother, a good friend, a minister, a colleague, a writer. I am enriched by my ethnic identity, clear about my sexual orientation, and I have always easily flowed both into my tears, and into a speechless ecstasy under any clear night sky silvered with stars.

But my experience of grief flows through every one of these other identities.

There are few academic classes about grief that I know of, and many of these are found only in seminaries, or as part of psychological curricula. Even then, the practical aspects of conducting a memorial or interpreting a crisis may receive more attention than the emotional palette of grief, its shades, hues, and contrasts.

Over many decades, however, I studied at the "school of hard knocks," a phrase my parents frequently used. The loss of my beloved grandparents, the loss of work friends to car accidents, and the loss of the greatest portion of my friends during the AIDS era in San Francisco were tough lessons.

I also learned that grief was not simply death's companion, but that it touched every aspect of my life. I grieved when I moved away from my childhood home in Detroit to California, so far from my beloved grandparents. How I wince when I remember my grandmother's loving face turned into a distorted image—a living Picasso portrait—when she hugged me goodbye, and would not let me go. On a very different level, I grieved when a painting of mine was stolen off the display wall in a gallery. I have grieved when deep relationships of either friendship or romantic love ended. The first time I experienced a broken heart I freely wondered how so-called civilization had survived as long as it has if such a pain is common. Nothing in my life made much sense after such losses. I began to wonder what part unacknowledged grief has played in wars, claims of entitlement, class segregation, and the systemic violence always tightening its grip around people of color, sexual minorities, and women.

I came to understand that the word *grief*, like the word *color*, serves as a handy abstraction rather than an expression of anything precise.

As a pastel artist, I know in my bones that although forest green and gold are both colors, they are wildly different from each other, both in the feelings they evoke and the associations they offer both heart and eye.

And the school of hard knocks has taught me over the years that grief is like that word *color* because it has a variety of authentic meanings. Some of these meanings blend, some don't. As an artist, I can blend certain blues and yellows to create a rich green, but sometimes, a pure unblended crimson is what works best on the canvas.

In a similar way, as a griever for six decades, I might dwell for a long time after a loss in sorrow, or anger, or regret, or I might move on to more transformative aspects of the grieving process. But all of these hues and shades of grief are truly, if abstractly, contained within the single-syllable word, *grief*.

Robert Frost titled his poem "Nothing Gold Can Stay," and he concludes its colorful beauty with the same line. Nothing of whatever form, of whatever color—gold, green, crimson—can stay. Not one thing lasts forever. No one lasts forever. It *all* goes, as life flows on. Yet color itself, and new forms, new life, will process into being. Persons—but not us—will still walk the earth centuries hence.

The generations fall and new ones rise. In the same way, beautiful colors in a modern painting by Georgia O'Keefe delight, even as the ancient colors Leonardo Da Vinci daubed onto the wet wall bearing his "Last Supper" deteriorate, visible only by the memory called restoration. Thus, I can strongly affirm that beauty and life still exist *side by side* with loss and grief. As poet Kevin Young puts it so splendidly,

Grief might be easy
if there wasn't still
such beauty—would be far
easier if the silver

maple didn't thrust
its leaves into flame

The contrast between being dazzled by the beauty of the world, and at the same time, isolated by desolation, has always deepened both such experiences in my life. I love the beauty more, I feel the grief more keenly.

Or as Louise Glück says with serene economy: "The love of form is a love of endings."

And poet Albert Huffstickler gives us some idea what happens when, in loving the forms of this world, we also feel their loss:

Let the pain be the pain
not in the hope that it will vanish
but in the faith that it will fit in.

All of my life, I have been trying to fit the pain of grief into the shape of my whole life so that it nestles against all the other forms that make up the mosaic of me: my capacity to love deeply, my risk-taking, my self-doubts, my questions, my book and experiential knowledge, my fear, and even my physical health.

And I have been trying to fit the shape of grief into my days since very early in my life.

My cousin Linda had been diagnosed with leukemia when she was three. I didn't know what that meant, of course, since she and I were about the same age. I'm not sure that she understood what that meant either, except for lots of trips to the doctor, and large white-tiled hospitals with glaring lights and too many needles.

I don't remember either of my parents sitting down to talk to me about it, although I do remember they both sighed a lot when they spoke of her. I remember that their sighs prompted a kind of dread in me.

I was a kindergartener at Columbus School, across from our bungalow on Springarden Street on the East Side of Detroit. My mother would watch me cross the street in the morning. In the afternoon, I usually walked back across the street by myself, after playing with friends for about a half hour as we climbed the ladder of branches in one of the large pine trees by the side of the school. I knew enough, of course, never to tell my mother what I had been doing.

One day, after school and play, I entered the side door, as usual, walked through the little kitchen of our bungalow, and into the living room. My mother was sitting on the couch, off to one side. She didn't say hello, she just stared at me, silently. I didn't say hello to her either. I stopped in my tracks. Then I spoke these words: "Linda died, didn't she?"

My mother nodded almost imperceptibly, and suddenly, tears erupted from my eyes, and my whole body shook. Then I bolted to her and threw myself in her lap. She held me as I cried. Whether her eyes overflowed then I don't remember. But I remembered for years my own tears and the trembling in my body. It was a bit scary to me that my whole body could just suddenly detonate like that, shuddering with feelings it could barely contain.

Fifty-five years later when I mentioned this formative event to my mother, she had no memory of it. Her grief at the time was different perhaps, affecting her memory in a different way than my own

But I learned something the day Linda died. I learned that my *body* knows things, sometimes as much as my head and heart.

I do count that day as my first experience of grief, at least that I remember. There were other times I had to face loss. One was less dramatic, because it involved a thing, not a person; someone stole my bike. My grief then took the form of anger, not tears. Anger at the thief, whoever it may have been, and anger at myself for letting it get out of my sight.

I felt what I now know as grief when I changed schools, or a favorite teacher moved away. A woman whose lawn I used to trim took her own life after her husband died. I remember my mother sitting me down to explain that to me as best she could. But I really didn't know her well, so my grief took the form of wondering how sad a person would have to be to take their own life. I wondered, "Would *I* ever be that sad when I got older?"

Of course, almost six decades later, the experiences of grief and loss in my life have defined it and shaped it in ways I would never have known. I am a child of grief as much as gratitude, joy, and love. And as far as I know, through thirty-five years of ministerial experience, grief is also part of every human life. And I've even come to think that other animals on this earth experience forms of grief as well.

This book is a personal exploration of one of the few realities other than breath, water, nourishment, and mortality that unites all seven billion of us into a singular humanity. And I am not just reflecting on grief for death, but also for every sort of loss in our lives.

Grief is so deeply personal in every case that it almost makes no sense to speak of its universality, at least without incorporating the purely personal. The oft-told Buddhist story of Siddhartha Gautama and Kisa Gotami illumines this paradox well:

When the fiercely grieving mother Kisa Gotami comes to the revered Siddhartha and begs him to raise her dead child back to life, he refuses at first. But since she will not relent her imploring, he offers to work the magic if only she will provide for him a certain kind of mustard seed, found only in the homes of families never visited by death and grief. Kisa Gotami goes from house to house, family to family, but of course, cannot find the life-restoring seed. She helps comfort the families, cooks for them, reaches out to them in *their* grief. She then realizes that mortality is the universal reality, and returns to her teacher, wiser. Together, she and Siddhartha bury her dead child. And, enlightened by her realization, Kisa Gotami goes on to become a very wise nun and even an *arhat*, a venerated saint.

The paradox illustrated by this story does not destroy, but rather deepens each affirmation—the uniquely personal reality of grief, and the uniting universality of it. It's as if personal compassion shares some aspect of the communal for a time.

In the same way, these pages, rooted in the deeply personal, open into private use and meditation, but they may also be useful in gatherings of individuals as well, such as grief circles within congregations or small group ministry circles, by whatever name.

Although certainly children experience grief (as I did when my cousin Linda died), these reflections are written primarily for those who have been reflecting on loss in their longer lives. I record times of great personal sadness, but I have not found sadness during the writing of these reflections, only a gratefulness that grief has so many rich colors, shades, and hues; and that, in general, all these colors serve deep human needs. They articulate some of the best meanings of what it means to be human. Nothing to be ashamed of, explained away, hidden, or denied. Refusing to embrace grief in all its richness is like deciding to hold our breath to live more fully, or pretending we are not thirsty when we are. It really makes little sense to avoid this gift, which I might even call a spiritual gift or path.

Psychologist David Richo describes a spiritual path as our commitment "to constantly shed our illusions." Thus, the stories of grief in our lives call us to an inescapable spiritual path, a journey which each of us will take for rest of our days.

Best, I've come to feel, if we journey together sometimes. . . .

grief

and sorrow

I had been sitting *shiva* for my best friend, Stephen (pro-
nounced Stef'n), at the home he shared with his partner, Richard. It was day number five of that intriguing
Jewish custom of staying home for a week after a death
in the family. You cover the mirrors, neglect things like
shaving, and in the evening people bring food and the
spiritual nourishment of ritual.

The kitchen table was heaped with lavish dishes. People came into the kitchen, put food on their plates, and
walked off, carrying their dishes into the other rooms to
talk and console each other. Plates had piled up from the
various visitors nibbling throughout the day, so I started
to wash some of them in the large oval sink. Only a few
people were still in the kitchen. I was stacking the various plates, organizing the casserole dishes, and sorting

the silverware as the water running from the tap grew hot. I had wanted something to do. Suddenly, my hands in soapy water filling the sink, I broke down. I mean, I really broke down. The sobbing shot out of me like a rocket. I didn't feel it coming; it just erupted. Suddenly. No warning. My shoulders heaved. My wail was heard in the next room. A member of the synagogue came in and laid his hand on my heaving shoulder.

"Are you alright?" he asked.

"I'm okay. This sobbing is what okay looks like for me now. I suddenly realized how much I miss Stephen and I cannot believe I will never see him again. I'm just so sad."

"I see," he said. "Of course." And he left me alone to cry in my public yet totally private domain.

Sorrow is one of the most prominent aspects of grief. The tears and sobbing. The shock and wailing. I remember the first time I saw Picasso's most effective painting, *Guernica*, in the New York Museum of Modern Art. I almost burst into tears, even though I wasn't mourning anyone in particular at the time. The wailing woman depicted on the left side of the canvas, holding her dead child in her arms, her neck stretched to the pinnacle of sorrow, hit me like a hammer and tears flowed from my eyes.

Sorrow is desolation and beyond easy comforting. Even if it's not an eruption of tears and cries, even if it's expressed with reserve, sorrow is the feeling of unacceptable loss at the heart of all grieving. It's a form of disbelief in the reality of the loss, a refusal, a lightning bolt suddenly striking sharply to clearly light up the impossibility of the loss.

I have held many people in my arms, and have been held myself in moments of sorrow: in mutual bodily witness to the mourning of a young man's death in a distant war or the death of a best friend or a beloved spouse who died young because of an untreatable illness or an accident or a murder or a medical mishap.

And sometimes, yes, I do *not* want to be held. I want to be alone by myself. No one else can understand. No one else has been where I have been.

True. But not *entirely* true, of course.

Sorrow sometimes ebbs into depression or simply fades with time into something less thoroughly present and totally occupying. But for me, it is often the principal gateway to all the other aspects of grief.

grief
and weariness

I lived in the San Francisco Bay Area for twenty-four years. In 1981 I remember reading the *New York Times* thoroughly one summer day as I rode the subway. Somewhere way in the back pages I saw an article reporting that a number of young men were suffering from Kaposi's sarcoma, a rare cancer usually found only in older men with Mediterranean heritage. The only thing those young men had in common was same-gender sexual activity. I clearly remember actually saying aloud in the crowded subway car, "*Now* what?"

I found out "what." As did pretty much everyone in the Bay Area within a short time. The abbreviation HLTV was the first of many attempts to explain why these young men were experiencing these unusual symptoms and dying so young. The next abbreviation was AIDS, and finally HIV.

Over the next decade, I lost friend after friend after friend. When my best friend, Stephen, told me that he had tested positive for HIV, I kept my feelings within me as he talked and I listened. After all, others were in the room when he called. Then when we ended the phone conversation, I went into my room, closed the door, and threw myself onto my pillow and sobbed bitterly. In those days, before the medications available now, such news almost always meant an early death.

I officiated at the memorial services for many friends. When Stephen died, I fell apart for a good long time. Nothing was right about the world. Medicines to treat HIV came out not long after Stephen was laid to rest, but the fact that they came out too late to save him meant that I didn't focus much on news about the latest treatments.

Go forward ten years. Stephen's surviving partner and my close friend, Richard, called me up one day and said, cheerily, "Guess what, Mark?"

"I don't know, what?"

"The sky is blue, the grass is green."

"Yes, true," I said, knowing he was building up to something. "And robins have red breasts. So, um, what are you saying, Richard?"

"Do you realize that it's been ten years since Stephen died? Since anyone we've known who has HIV died?"

"I guess I hadn't thought about that. But you're right."

"You and I and all those who supported us in those days were in the trenches for a long time back in the 1980s and early 1990s. Like in the First World War. Shells exploding over us, cries of terror, our friends dying all around us. I've just noticed recently that it's gotten quiet, so I dared to poke my head above the top of the trench, and guess what I saw?"

"What?"

"Everyone else had been shopping down at the mall the whole time."

I laughed. But I recognized with my laugh that *I* was feeling different too. And of course, Richard expressed this different feeling with his usual wit, and I remembered that it was not just gay men whose weariness was lifting. It was lifting for all the lesbians and other allies of every orientation who had been making meals, driving people to hospitals, and learning how to conduct honest funerals in a world in which the status quo of the time balked against such honesty.

I said to Richard, "I feel like I have been weary to the bone for almost two decades. Memorials almost every weekend. Not a day went by when I didn't open the newspaper and see the face of someone I used to know—and often cared about—in the obituaries. I just shut down so many parts of my soul. I feel like I am recovering and opening my soul so that it once again can move through the world with openness and gratitude."

Our reflective conversation describes one aspect of the weariness associated with grief. Grief can arrive on our shores not as a wave but as a series of tsunamis.

A woman in the congregation I serve recently reminded me of something else I have experienced with grief: weariness in the form of sheer bodily exhaustion. Sobbing takes it out of you physically. It works the muscles and alters the breath. It tires the bones. The whole effort to focus on the ordinary needs of life—food, laundry, and so forth—in the midst of grief can feel as though you had just spent three hours running a course or lifting weights in the gym. In the weeks after Stephen died I remember how frequently I would fall asleep simply sitting up in a chair. I deliberately made taking naps as much a part of my day as eating supper or brushing my teeth, even if I had managed to sleep deeply the night before.

Grief has often worn me out, while restoring me to myself at the same time.

But the one does not seem to come without the other.

interlude

Redemption Song

Finally fall.
At last the mist,
heat's haze, we woke
these past weeks with

has lifted. We find
ourselves chill, a briskness
we hug ourselves in.
Frost greying the ground.

Grief might be easy
if there wasn't still
such beauty—would be far
simpler if the silver

maple didn't thrust
its leaves into flame,

trusting that spring
will find it again.

All this might be easier if
there wasn't a song
still lifting us above it,
if wind didn't trouble

my mind like water.
I half expect to see you
fill the autumn air
like breath—

At night I sleep
on clenched fists.
Days I'm like the child
who on the playground

falls, crying
not so much from pain
as surprise.
I'm tired of tide

taking you away,
then back again—
what's worse, the forgetting
or the thing

you can't forget.
Neither yet—
last summer's
choir of crickets

grown quiet.

—Kevin Young

grief

and ritual

When my best friend, Stephen, died, he was already on the road to converting to Judaism, the religious practice of his partner, Richard. So Richard and I buried him according to the Jewish traditions of Sha'ar Zahav, the San Francisco synagogue I often attended with the two of them on Friday nights.

Although we knew the basic vocabulary—Richard more than me, of course—the rabbi helped us relate more deeply to the Jewish grief rituals. At the time of Stephen's death, at which we both were present, we became *shomerim*, that is, guardians. We stayed with Stephen's body until it was taken to the Jewish mortuary across the street. The rabbi instructed us on the tradition: we were neither to eat nor drink nor even pray until the body was taken from the room where we sat by it. These directions startled me at first, until I heard Richard sigh, "O rabbi, rabbi, you have come to bring order into the disorder of this day."

Later that day we spoke with the rabbi in his office. He reminded us that until the actual burial, we were *onen*, that is, people in a state of *aninut*, or shock, and that we should be merciful to ourselves, because we might find ourselves speaking abruptly or withdrawing in ways different from our ordinary selves. On Friday morning, Richard and I accompanied members of the synagogue, Richard's cousins, and our friends to the Jewish cemetery at Colma, outside San Francisco. The rabbi had asked both Richard and me to bring two sturdy friends as our support. I didn't understand how literally he meant that. I asked my friend Tom to be there for me.

A deep hole had been dug, and we gathered around it. A mountain of freshly turned soil sat next to one end of the grave. The simple wooden coffin had already been placed at the bottom of the hole.

The rabbi instructed our two chosen friends to come behind Richard and me as we stood at the edge of the hole and to place their hands on our backs. Then the rabbi asked the others to place their hands on the backs of our two friends, and the two of us were to lean back and be supported.

The experience was remarkable, and it underscored for me the tangible power of community. The rabbi said a few words, and I told a central story about the beautiful relationship Stephen and I had enjoyed, and I wept. A few others spoke. I was supported the entire time. Physically. Spiritually. Emotionally. At the end of the funeral, our friends put Richard and me more squarely on our feet. We took up the shovels on hand and shoveled some of the soil into the grave to rattle on the coffin. Others joined in, and we literally buried him.

That day was among the more moving days of my whole life. Partially because of the artfulness and power of the ritual, one I had not known before. Now I know that ritual benefits from repetition, it deepens, layer after layer; and each time a mourning prayer is said—the well-known Kaddish, for example—within the Jewish community, it has the power to connect one death with all others, offering a poignant insight into the universality of mortality. But even without that religious history in my blood, the ritual did its good work. As did the week of *shiva*, or housebound, daytime solitude, and evening prayers. Saying the Kaddish prayer so frequently helped my grieving heart, no matter that it's in Aramaic, a language I do not speak. But I was especially moved by the singular ritual at the graveside, entirely new to me, but powerful.

It's possible that the sung ritual words I *did* grow up with, the staccato and tender *Requiem aeternam* (eternal rest) of my youth, had reserved a spacious place in my heart, because a repeated ritual works more deeply. I don't know. I do find myself listening to recorded musical requiems when a friend dies, no matter their religion or lack of it.

I have come to understand that the memorials I have led in congregations are also times of ritual, even if Latin or Aramaic are not used. Sacred storytelling, I call it. The ritual I have used throughout my ministry unfolds the meaning of the ancient Greek word *anamnesis*, "to make present again."

In this ritual I share significant stories from the life of one who has died, using vivid detail supplied by the family and often by my own memory, and then woven by me into a retelling, always in present tense. Others present may tell individual stories and disclose memories, but I usually offer the complete overview of the person's life. It's often more than a eulogy—another Greek word, meaning "good words"—because, where fitting, even the tougher stories that reveal the fullness of a human life are often there right beside the good words of praise and thanks.

I remember once talking about a man's rough struggle with alcoholism, his family finding him under the kitchen table in the morning, sleeping it off. This sadness was part of his life, mixed with his kindness, his fatherly affection, and his skillful work. His family wisely encouraged me to hold nothing back. One family friend said to me afterward, in surprise, "Oh my God, you actually talked about him under the table. I knew that, but you actually told the truth aloud, along with all the other truths of his life. Thank you. I felt relieved that you mentioned it. I paid closer attention to what you said after you did that."

We often know more about each other than what we say, and our lives deeply touch the lives around us. No one's life makes complete sense out of that context and outside the embrace of thoughtful honesty.

The ritual of the services I have crafted does not have one singular indispensable prayer or psalm. No Kaddish, no *Requiem aeternam*, not even the great favorite in many Protestant churches, Psalm 23, "The Lord is my shepherd." I have used all these texts of course, when the religious roots and practices of the mourners are complex and blended. I have used newer translations of Psalm 23 as well, and Marcia Falk's great rewrite of the Kaddish based on a poem by Zelda. I freely use non-traditional words that link life and truthfulness with love and compassion, context and care. One simple text I use often is H. Donald Johnston's "In the presence of life we say no to death, in the presence of death, we say yes to life."

But I've come to believe that some ritual at the time of death is significant for the griever. Leora, a woman in her nineties, came up to me after a memorial she had just attended. She told me that she didn't want any kind of service, because she wasn't important enough to have all the fuss made. I said, "Not important enough? Well, Leora, you are important to me! You are important to the whole

congregation! You are important to your whole family!"
(Oh my God, was she a remarkable person, a veritable
Norma Rae in the labor movement of the 1930s!)

"Leora, the service I would do would not be 'fussy,'
I promise, but the service is not for you. No, it's for all
of us. The world will be different without you in it, and
we need to acknowledge that, and that we will miss you,
and that our lives were changed for good because of
you. Besides (I said with a playful wink to balance the
tender feeling building up in me), are you going to come
back and haunt me if I do a service for you anyway?"

She smiled, and then laughed and said, "Well, since
you put it that way, go ahead. But a *simple* fuss, okay?"

"Okay," I said. And that's indeed what I did.

The word *ritual* is often confused with particular rituals, as if only one real form exists. For example, my
friend Dallas died at age thirty-two of insulin shock. He
had never once told me he was diabetic. I knew him as
an artist and as an overworked registered nurse. A fellow
Detroiter by birth, he was also a trained body worker, a
superb dancer, and a print model. We connected about
his art a lot, but I also shared a unique relationship with
him. We were grief partners. Three of his six brothers
had been murdered in Detroit over a period of three
years. My closest friends were all dying of HIV. So we
comforted each other by talking about our deep feelings
and anguish, and we did this many times. I was always
grateful for time with him.

His death stunned me. Age thirty-two and gone. I read about it in the obituaries, completely surprised by the news of his type 1 diabetes. So I decided to go to his memorial, held in a school building on Valencia Street in San Francisco and led by some of his friends. The form of the ritual was unexpected. With no welcome or beginning that I could understand, I suddenly heard long readings from Trotsky and Lenin about workers. Turns out that Dallas had been politically active in a small communist organization, yet another thing I didn't know about him. Reading after reading went by until I raised my hand and asked if someone could talk about other aspects of his life, the nursing, the dancing, the hundred beautiful charcoal drawings he created that wallpapered his apartment.

So a conversation began, threaded with individual memories. No one else quite knew him as an artist like I did. Few knew that he danced with all the grace of a professional, always by himself on the dance floor of some club. Only some knew some of his nursing stories, and hardly anyone knew about his murdered brothers.

So in the schoolroom that day, the ritual that comforts me, talking about the life of a loved one with tenderness, joined the ritual of readings from Trotsky that comforted his political compatriots. At the end, all of us left empowered by the rituals that made sense to us, and that gave form and shape and context to our grief.

And so you will not be surprised that each year on February 14, and even though I am a Unitarian Universalist minister, not a rabbi, I light the *yahrzeit* (anniversary) candle and recite the Kaddish for Stephen, who died in 1995. Even so many years later, ritual gives form to grief.

grief

and theology

Over the years, I have felt privileged to hear many people talk about their understanding of the vast and sometimes ancient set of ideas we hold together in English with the single small syllable *God*.

I have heard in detail how experiences of disappointment, loss, and rational criticism dissolved that word for some, a word that often meant so much in their childhood. Now they can no longer bear to even hear it.

I have heard people speak of that word's deep meaning illuminating and transforming their present spiritual life, although I have yet to hear any two people say quite the same thing about what that means. I've known a surprising number of folks who do not use the word *God*, because it has never made sense to them since childhood. They did not so much lose their creed as never have one in the first place. I have heard people speak of the cosmos itself as God, and others who pray to God even though they claim agnosticism as their theological approach. I've known quite a few religious liberals to assert that God is no less than a symbol for awe and wonder, or "love and truth," to quote John in the New Testament. Or G-d as nothing, literally No Thing, according to one strand of the Hebrew scriptures, which the nontheist Jewish psychotherapist Erich Fromm rendered as the Nameless, an upside-down form of the traditional Ha-Shem, the Name. "I am becoming what I am becoming," Erich Fromm renders the Hebrew dynamically, verbally, rather than the statically and bizarrely translated "I am that I am" found in the King James translation. The Ultimate is best understood as Goddess, say many who claim a less distorted patriarchal history of the world. God becomes the spirit of life for some modern religious progressives, something difficult to illustrate, but deeply comforting, especially when sung in the hymn "Spirit of Life." God is Father and Mother said Theodore Parker in the nineteenth century. God is one's ultimate concern, according to Paul Tillich in the twentieth century. "God is doing, not being," says one twenty-first-century Kabbalist. "Resistance to tyranny is obedience to God," Susan B. Anthony once opined, suggesting that divinity is the spirit of defiance within human beings. For many religious communities with a history of oppression, such as African-American congregations or Metropolitan Community Churches, philosophical debates about God's existence evaporated long ago for the passionate affirmation of God as liberator, God as immanent comfort, God as promise of release from systems of diminishment which have distorted all reality. "To believe in god is to believe that something, somewhere is not stupid," concludes poet Joseph Pintauro, with a flourish.

I have moved through almost all these ideas in my life. Some of them tug at me still. But nearly all these notions evaporate when I read and re-read the lines from Elie Wiesel's great autobiography *Night*. Wiesel describes the execution of three human beings in a concentration camp during the Second World War, one of them a child:

> Then came the march past the victims. The two men were no longer alive. Their tongues were hanging out, swollen and bluish. But the third rope was still moving: the child, too light, was still breathing. . . . And so he remained for more than half an hour, lingering between life and death, writhing before our eyes. And we were forced to look at him at close range. He was still alive when I passed him. His tongue was still red, his eyes not yet extinguished.
>
> Behind me, I heard the same man asking:
> "For God's sake, where is God?"

And from within me, I heard a voice answer:

"Where is He? This is where—hanging here from this gallows."

When I was in Jerusalem once with my friend Ned, while we waited to check into the hotel we noticed a great arched window at the end of the lobby. The hotel was on the sixth floor of a building that poured down a cliff under that window to the first floor, a floor still high above the valley below. The view from the window was undeniably beautiful. The great golden wall of the old city off to the left, a large cliff with shallow caves to the right, distant whitewashed houses far away on the other side. But the ravine, right in the middle of the city, was wild. Trees, bushes, rocks—even a shepherd with a flock! We unfolded our map, trying to figure out where we were in the tangle of the city, and after a difficult search, we realized we were looking at Gehenna, the "Valley of the Hinnom Clan." In ancient times, we remembered, people believed that children were burned in sacrifice in temples there dedicated to deities from other nations. So they left that degraded site undeveloped once a later generation had torn those fiery altars down. At most, thereafter, people burned their trash there. Thus, later, in rabbinic times, Gehenna served as a synonym for utter loss and degradation, symbolically "hell." Christians in the Hellenistic era eventually revised the metaphor into a theological reality.

Ned and I decided to delay checking in and go explore. We carefully climbed down the precipitous cliff and came to the bottom of the deep ravine, the great golden wall high above us now. The bushes and undergrowth were close to the ground. Tangled in their curly roots were copious stones, spark plugs, carburetor parts, and paper cups from fast-food joints. It was still a garbage dump, as it had been in the days of Jesus, who metaphorically referred to the fires in Gehenna burning the refuse dumped there. (Our Universalist ancestors, excellent biblical scholars, clearly understood that Gehenna did not refer to the later theological horror of some everlasting place of torment that, centuries later, made its way into Christian teaching as official doctrine.)

From up above, the ravine was beautiful and green. Seen up close, it was ugly and disappointing.

However, something in the distance caught our eye. At the base of the stone cliff that anchored our hotel high above us was a black doorway of some kind. Curious, we made our way through the tangled vines and spark plugs to see what it was. As we got closer, we both recognized it as a first century tomb, for there in front of the dark doorway was a grooved track carved in stone and a large stone disc still there for the rolling. Both Ned and I had studied enough to know that only first-century tombs were constructed thus, and we found it exciting to see an archeological site not completely fenced off by rules and regulations of "Keep Away," albeit understandable rules and regulations. Above the tomb, carved in the stone, was a tablet with faded Greek letters from a much later time. We could make out the Greek word ἀνάστασις, *anastasis*, which means "to stand up again" in the Greek testament but is more often translated as "resurrection" in the English version of the scriptures. This first-century tomb had obviously been used by Greek-speaking Christians in the area centuries after it had been hollowed out of the cliff.

I proposed entering, but Ned wisely suggested that because we could not see inside at all, it might be wise to throw some rocks in and make noise. Who knew if some wild dogs might be inside? We did so, and we heard nothing, so we cautiously and slowly entered the rectangular entrance. It took several minutes for our eyes to adjust to the deep darkness since it was so bright outside by contrast. After a while, we could make out another door. We were only in the antechamber, not the tomb itself. Another door led into an even darker chamber where carved into the walls were the shelves on which the bodies would have been laid.

We decided to enter the next room, and this time it took almost five minutes for our pupils to open wide enough to see anything, however dim. We both saw it at the same time. Some cloths carefully folded up on one of the shelves. One of us, I don't remember who, said, "What is this? Are we in some Bible story? Is an angel nearby?" It was uncanny and startling. But then as our eyes adjusted even further, we saw that the clothes were blankets, and that on the floor before us were several worn but warm-looking sleeping bags and lots of crumpled McDonald's wrappers and a few leftover French fries. The tomb was a home for the homeless at night, the stone walls protection against cold winter nights in Jerusalem, which in February does indeed know snow and ice.

No standing up into new life. No resurrection. I felt deep grief as it dawned on me what we were seeing. Here in the city where prophets had witnessed for the plight of the poor and preached egalitarian economic messages, the homeless found their home in the cemeteries of the dead, on stone biers hidden in the dark. It was overwhelming. Ned and I talked about it for a while, mourning the absence of a culture in which we human beings proclaim to make caring for each other—in all our brokenness—our joyous spiritual practice. Instead, we found the gloomy evidence of a culture in which entire groups of people are disposable and delivered to their tombs long before their death.

To some, grieving for an unfulfilled vision of justice, equity, and compassion may not seem comparable to mourning the death of a loved one. But I found the ache in my heart quite similar. Theological imagery like the kind found in the too-often-literalized Easter story, or Elie Weisel's horrific experiential meditation, summon me to feel the larger grief for lives lost to the dominant paradigm of the haves and have-nots, the privileged and the nonprivileged, the them and the us. Without our grief as the first step, the first witness, I don't see how the dominant culture can be confronted. That which is ultimate—call it G-d or Love or Truth or the Spirit of Life or Great Nature or the Mystery—will have only tenuous power unless through us it gazes upon the gallows or notes who—blood of our blood and flesh of our flesh—lives in the tombs.

grief
and music

My friend John Zimarowski loved music of all kinds. He himself was a deft pianist. When I went to see him at his flat, he often would sit at his well-tuned piano and play some Ravel. *Gaspard de la nuit* was his consistent favorite. Our game was to have me suggest another composer, say, Leonard Bernstein. He would continue to play the Ravel, but add the jazzy syncopation that made *Candide* or *West Side Story* so exciting. The radiance of his soul and the radiance of music overlapped.

John was a well-rounded fellow. He vacationed in Bali every year, and returned home with new tropical dishes he would re-create in his own kitchen. I often watched him as he cooked. "This is *galangal*," he would teach, holding up something that looked like thin-skinned, pale ginger. "But they often call it *lengkuas.*"

He also crafted hilarious short stories that *Christopher Street* magazine loved to publish. I was privileged to hear him read his witty stories aloud before he sent them in to his editor, and they cracked me up every time. As John read lines from a scrawled manuscript, the crackling from burning logs in the fireplace added a bit of magic to the whole evening. He taught yoga (long before it was fashionable), made his living as a social worker, and left skit-like messages on his answering machine, which all of us who were privileged to call him friend dialed up every day for a reliable jolt of laughter.

John called me one day and told me he was extremely sick and that he was in the hospital. I immediately went to see him. I happened to be there when several doctors in white came in to tell him that he was suffering from HLTV, letters that meant what HIV means now, but that translated as AIDS. John was delirious and didn't quite understand. But I did. Then, sitting amid fifty other passengers as I went home on the Geary bus, I wept as quietly as I could. But I wept. In those days, it meant sure death.

John's Polish and Irish ancestry combined to give him a remarkable look: the bronze whorls of his hair, the gap between his front teeth, and best of all, his stunning translucent skin, which always looked as if light shone through it. Friends always mentioned his skin in particular, and asked him what he did to make it glow so.

Sadly, his skin was the first to go. In those days, full-blown AIDS was often preceded by what they used to call AIDS-related complex, or ARC. ARC showed itself in any one of several ways. For John, a terrible eczema covered his entire body. His beautiful skin became swollen and flaky, and he stayed indoors as much as possible where he would not see people recoil at his appearance.

One day John called me up and said, "They are playing your song." "Huh?" I asked.

"The symphony," he said. "Michael Tilson Thomas is going to conduct the *Glagolitic Mass* by Leos Janáček. You have always told me that was your single favorite piece of music, but I have never yet heard it. How about I get us some tickets so I can finally hear it?"

I was moved. He remembered that Janáček's great piece had helped me get through one of the most difficult times in my life, when I let go of everything I knew and set off without a map, for my heart's sake. The adamant "Amen!" in the *Slava* (or Gloria) section had held me aloft when I wanted to drop down and wither away. I thanked John for both the idea and the tickets. I was impressed that John had developed the confidence to go outside the shelter of his flat, although when he showed up at the symphony hall a few days later, he had his coat collar pulled high around his hat-covered head to disguise his face. When we were seated, I noticed that he had bought the best seats in the house.

It was a perfect performance in my book. The chorus was crisp, Thomas expertly balancing the pace. Afterward, I suddenly remembered that John had just heard this piece for the first time. "What if he didn't like it?" I wondered, horrified at the thought. I slowly turned to look at him. He turned to me slowly in return. His scaly skin was wet with his tears. His eyes were red. He said in his beautiful voice, "It was the most beautiful thing I have ever heard. It was completely life affirming, without any naiveté anywhere. When it comes time for me to die, I want to flow like that music flowed, not retreating but grateful for even the last minute of my life."

I knew at that moment I was on sacred ground. I wanted to take off my shoes, like Moses did before the fire in those branches. His words live in me to this day.

When he finally died, his partner, Jim, and I worked out the service, at the request of his mother. Jim said that John had wanted a tape played of Fred Astaire singing the famed song of the Gershwins' "They Can't Take That Away from Me." I was surprised, since John had never told me that it was his favorite song, nor had he ever played it on the piano. But of course, it was perfect, that music coinciding with my grief. As part of the service, I riffed on the lyrics, saying, "The gap between your teeth, the curl in your hair, the spice in your cuisine, your music in the air . . . No, you can't take that away from me."

Over the years, I have noted how often grief and music coincide. The rhythm of the Kaddish I have chanted for my Jewish friends propels my grief, even as it cradles it: *Yitgadal v'yitkadash sh'mei raba. B'alma di v'ra chirutei.* The Aramaic sounds have meaning, sure, but it's their sonority that comforts me. The old Latin requiem of my youth, which Maurice Duruflé took verbatim and enriched wondrously, still flows through my mind when I grieve. Songs I have shared with someone become more than memories. They are evocations of particular relationships, even if the liveliness of the music seems too cheerful or even wild to some. Sometimes when I lead a memorial, the family wants a song played that many outside the family would consider inappropriate. But over the years, I have been moved by how even idiosyncratic songs can sometimes bless grief. Jazz or rock favorites, Beatles' tunes, Bobby McFerrin's feminine version of Psalm 23, Jacques Brel's "If We Only Have Love," or Sting's great anthem "Fragile" have all worked with grief, not against it.

One day many years after John died, I chanced to be with two colleagues on the great beach of Point Reyes in Marin County. We came to eat lunch together and talk, "far from the madding crowd." They both brought their beloved dogs with them to run on the beach, and so, after our picnic, they left me alone for about half an hour on the empty beach. The sound of the surf rolling in with the tide was soothing and rhythmic. Suddenly, out of nowhere, John's image entered my consciousness, and I wondered why his memory had surged right at that moment. With gratitude I realized that the pounding surf echoed the sure rhythm of great music, and I realized my heart had imagined John playing the sea for me as once he had delighted me on his piano. A lovely moment to be sure, a poetic blossom of grief, but it was the power of music that blessed it.

grief

and depression

Four months after Stephen, my best friend, died, I went into a deep depression. Oh, I had wept plenty and went through some stages of grief that Elisabeth Kübler-Ross once outlined, and a few she didn't include in her theory too. But in May, one of her five stages settled in, and stayed. Week after week, I found getting out of bed in the morning almost impossible, as if anchors were holding down my limbs. I was totally depressed.

At the office everything seemed trivial to me: letters, meetings, parish problems. Social functions and even dinner with friends, all trivial, unequal to the grayness that stole all the color from my life.

At mid-afternoon I would often sleep or go home early. I would preach on Sundays, yes, but in those days I didn't spend time writing my sermons; I just crafted them on the spot, linking the readings I had chosen with a few stories. I was alive while I was leading worship—I could manage that—but the rest of the time I was a ghost.

The depression felt physical to me. I thought if someone drew my blood for a medical test, it would simply weigh three times more than usual. Everything inside me felt sluggish. The bright California sun, the sparkling East Bay sunlight no less, seemed wan and dusty. When people asked how I was, I would say, "Okay," but even then I knew I really never fooled anyone. I imagined they thought I was trying to reassure them that I was slogging through it.

But I wasn't. Some days I didn't want to live anymore. I had buried so many friends in the preceding years—Mark De Wolfe, Frank Siskowski, Alex Stevens, my beloved John Zimarowski—but I knew my depression was not just a cumulative thing but was grief for Stephen particularly.

Why live in a world without Stephen? I would ask myself. What kind of a world is that? Stupid world. Ridiculous world. Empty world.

I would lie there in my bed, the iridescent May sun outside delighting every other person but me, I imagined. I could think of a hundred reasons to get up, but only one to stay in bed, and that was the loss of Stephen. And so I stayed under the covers.

I spoke with a therapist, and then with a few good friends. I walked along the beach. I read the great poets, especially Rilke. By mid-June that year the depression began to ebb. I began to see Stephen's death as one with all others I had experienced, and somehow that larger view lifted me out of the trough of May into a summery light.

The Oakland sun thrilled me again as it splashed across the windows at Ratto's in downtown Oakland or painted Lake Merritt the perfect color of tangerines just before sunset. I felt grateful to be alive again. But since that day, when someone speaks of their depression, I immediately feel the physicality of those gloomy days and wonder if what I felt then resembles what they are feeling now.

But I am fortunate, I know now, that it lasted only a few months for me. And, as I said, though I am no longer depressed as I was, eighteen years later every February 14 I still light the *yahrzeit*, the anniversary candle, memorializing Stephen's death. The living flame reminds me of two things: the aliveness of my love and the reality that all things change, even Stephen, even me.

grief
and memory

Some people say that sometime after a death the memory loosens its grip on the tougher memories and focuses only on the more pleasant ones. While that may be true for some folks, in my years in the ministry I have witnessed many stories where the pain of family misery can be so great that the pleasant memories get lost, and the memory crystallizes around a knot of real and well-remembered misery.

But for two important people in my life neither of these two relationships between memory and grief apply.

My grandmother Anna lost *all* her memories for nearly sixteen years when Alzheimer's disease cloaked her mind for good. She could remember neither the unpleasant (the tragic death of her second child, Anita, still a baby, in a car wreck) nor the pleasant (her wonderful letters to relatives and friends, her sumptuous meals for them, her hospitality).

And one day I heard my other grandmother, Carmelina, recall her memories and I discovered an entirely different lens for considering the relationship between memory and grief.

I had returned to the Detroit area for the winter holidays. My grandmother was ninety years old. One particular afternoon I saw the door to her room open, and knocked on it, hoping to visit with her. She was sitting on her well-made bed. On the floor in front of her was a large chest I had never seen before. The lid was open and inside were quite literally thousands of photographs, not in any particular order and many of them obviously quite old. Most were black and white photos, with those fancy cut edges. Others were early color photos, now faded to a bronze abstraction.

She was looking at them, one at a time. I asked if I could sit with her, and she patted the place next to her.

"What are all these?" I asked.

"Memories," she answered. Then she held up a photo for me to see. A man of about fifty. A fedora on his head, sunlight strong on his simple, white cotton shirt.

"This is Giuseppe Burchi; we used to find good mushrooms with him down at Palmer Park. He died in 1978." I had never heard his name before and wondered how many people she had known whom I would never hear about.

She held up another photo. A woman. Claudia Magnani. Another person I didn't know. "She and I and Lazar (her nickname for my grandfather) used to play pinochle in the afternoons down on Maine Street. She used to live across Davidson and would walk over. She died in 1982."

My grandmother went on like this for some time. A photo, then a name, some known (like John Baba, their neighbor) and some unknown (Delfina Guerri, someone else from Fanano, her hometown in Emilia). With each name, she provided a one- or two-sentence identification, or a short story in some cases, concluding with the date of the person's death.

After forty-five minutes of this amazing litany, I grew more and more moved until I could no longer listen to her. I had to say something. "Grandma," I said, "oh my God, you have outlived everyone except your son and your grandchildren."

"I know," she responded right away, as if she was expecting me to say that. She turned her head to look at me over the top of her glasses, always the sign that she was about to say something memorable. "That's why, when people get to my age, they die."

Hearing her use the word *die* like that surprised me a bit. So I asked, "What do you mean?"

"Well, Marco, every time someone dies, a hole opens up in your heart. And it never closes, as far as I can tell. By the time you are ninety years old, all you have left is a big hole. So it's time to go."

She smiled a bit, I think because she saw some tears beginning to dampen my eyes, and she wanted to let me know she was okay. "I have lived a good life, and have many good memories as well as hard memories. But it has been my life. And I am glad to have lived it."

I am sure that other things happened that day, or even that holiday week. But I have a hard time remembering what they were.

grief

and focus

Over the years as I have talked with those who are grieving, and as I have observed myself go through that process, I've noticed that a major expression of grief is a sustained inability to focus.

When I am in this state, I find I cannot follow through, I cannot keep commitments and routines that normally order and structure my life. All of a sudden they seem a bit empty, vague, and even pointless. Even when a friend calls me up to try and "distract" me because I am grieving, I find that I don't need to be distracted by anyone—*everything* is distracting! Although I appreciate the kindness, I often just stay in by myself. My thoughts tumble, follow no coherent course; my feelings derail easily. I can be talking with someone I dearly love and suddenly lose track of the entire conversation. I take in the words, but they glance off something protective on the inside and drift away. Nothing grabs me for long. Nothing keeps me on track.

This lack of focus endures long or passes swiftly, and some people are far less affected by it than others. Perhaps it dances with distinct personality norms already in place, thus taking slightly different forms within distinct hearts. I have experienced losing focus about nearly everything, except for one thing that dominates my focus completely. After my partner of sixteen years and I ended our relationship, I figured the service the next Sunday would be a complete disaster, because I was so upset and because in those days I preached without notes. But my sermon flowed far better than it had in months. Although I could focus on nothing else during that time, I focused on my Sunday sermon with the precision of the Hubble lens translating the misty light of a distant star into meaningful clarity. This took me by complete surprise. Nothing else mattered, however, and for a month or so I was simply "not there." Except in the pulpit, I was just going through the motions.

This state of unfocused perception serves a healing function, I believe. It isn't anything to fear, although it certainly can be confusing and disruptive. I've come to see it as the way the grieving heart forms a cocoon around itself. This cocoon creates a delicate but real spaciousness separated from the demands and duties and worries and relentless schedules of modern-day life.

It takes room to grieve, room that our frantic, confusing, and narcissistic modern world refuses to notice or offer. I am glad that our hearts can create the room that we need.

interlude

Celestial Music

I have a friend who still believes in heaven.
Not a stupid person, yet with all she knows, she literally
    talks to god,
she thinks someone listens in heaven.
On earth, she's unusually competent.
Brave, too, able to face unpleasantness.

We found a caterpillar dying in the dirt, greedy ants
    crawling over it.
I'm always moved by weakness, by disaster, always
    eager to oppose vitality.
But timid, also, quick to shut my eyes.
Whereas my friend was able to watch, to let events play
    out
according to nature. For my sake, she intervened,
brushing a few ants off the torn thing, and set it down
    across the road.

My friend says I shut my eyes to god, that nothing else
    explains
my aversion to reality. She says I'm like the child who
    buries her head in the pillow
so as not to see, the child who tells herself
that light causes sadness—
My friend is like the mother. Patient, urging me
to wake up an adult like herself, a courageous person—

In my dreams, my friend reproaches me. We're walking
on the same road, except it's winter now;
she's telling me that when you love the world you hear
    celestial music:
look up, she says. When I look up, nothing.
Only clouds, snow, a white business in the trees
like brides leaping to a great height—
Then I'm afraid for her; I see her
caught in a net deliberately cast over the earth—

In reality, we sit by the side of the road, watching the
    sun set;
from time to time, the silence pierced by a birdcall.
It's this moment we're both trying to explain, the fact
that we're at ease with death, with solitude.
My friend draws a circle in the dirt; inside, the
    caterpillar doesn't move.

She's always trying to make something whole,
    something beautiful, an image
capable of life apart from her.
We're very quiet. It's peaceful sitting here, not speaking,
    the composition
fixed, the road turning suddenly dark, the air
going cool, here and there the rocks shining and
    glittering—
it's this stillness that we both love.
The love of form is a love of endings.

—Louise Glück

grief
and animals

Over my decades as a minister, some of my most powerful grief conversations have been with people who have lost beloved pets. Dogs who had been companions for fifteen years, wagging their tails in unflagging affection. Cats who purred for twenty years on laps. Birds who sang themselves into their owners' hearts for twenty-five years.

I have done ceremonies for some pets, complete with readings, that have often brought solace to those who loved the animal. Some pet owners are ridiculed for openly grieving the loss of their pets, I've heard tell, but I haven't met anyone for whom such rude dismissiveness shamed them into not grieving.

Grief for pets is one with the larger circles of grief that most of us enter at some time in our lives. My career in ministry has convinced me that grieving for pets who have died is not trivial. For some who live alone, pets have been companions. For some who are ill, pets can provide comfort and healing far more effectively than handfuls of pills.

I understand how folks who make seasonal costumes for their pets or spend thousands on grooming them are perceived as "going too far" by some who do not enjoy such a presence in their homes. But for me, even such elaborate and sometimes playful excess demonstrates the extraordinary power of pets in people's lives.

When I was a freshman in high school my pet parakeet, Jerry, died. My tears ran quick and hot when my mother told me as we were driving home from school. She was sad with me, because she liked the singing and chirping while she was ironing next to Jerry's cage. We both grieved.

But animals and grief have another connection, at least for some of us. After my friend Stephen died, I went through a period of unexpected ecstasy. I was happy and cheerful all the time, almost annoyingly so, according to some friends. I felt alive, attuned to everything around me. Each rose, each star felt like an overwhelming gift.

I shared this with a beloved colleague at a collegial gathering. I also recounted my experiences with the Jewish ritual approach to death. My friend responded, "Do you have any animal stories?"

For a few seconds I was totally confused. "Animal stories?" Then I remembered something. While we were sitting *shiva* for Stephen, five days into it the weather outside was so perfect, so bright, so clear that we decided to take a little break from the house, to exercise a bit by taking a walk. It was an aid to our grieving in fact, a reminder that the world was out there still, no matter how enclosed we felt by our sense of loss.

San Francisco has some steep streets and sidewalks. Some sidewalks slant like stair cases. As Richard and I climbed one of those ramp-like sidewalks that day, trudging past a garage, a beautiful black cat jumped out in front of us. The cat looked up at Richard and me, and then walked a figure eight around our legs, passing between us. It did this three times. Then it paused between us, looked up at us, back and forth, back and forth, then suddenly darted away so fast that it was beyond our view in seconds. Baffled by this totally out-of-the-blue strangeness, we looked at each other, as Richard asked, "Stephen?"

We both giggled a bit, brightening in delight. But we also suddenly felt solemn, almost as if the experience with the cat refocused out attention on what we had been doing all week: grieving.

Now, when some folks hear this story they leap to unwarranted assumptions framed in questions: Did Richard and I suddenly lose our sense and "believe" that Stephen, upon his death, had transmigrated to a beautiful cat (which was already five years old, at least)? Did we believe that Stephen was sending us signals from beyond the grave? Rapping at the table of life with luminous cat eyes? Things like that?

Mostly I just roll my eyes a bit and refuse to enter the metaphysical fray. I have long ago stopped trying to link specific theological or philosophical constructs to marvelous events in my life. I have no final answers to offer about death, although I admit I have never found any reason to regard eternal hellfire as anything but the last socially permitted act of terrorism toward children. So I guess I am pretty clear about something. But a black cat on a sidewalk staring up at two grieving partners?

This encounter with the cat was clearly also a part of our grief. One experience among many. A bout of tears, a silent afternoon, a fit of anger, an animal encounter; all part of the flow of grief, not an invitation to a particular theological view.

I sometimes say to folks who are deeply grieving the loss of a spouse, "Everything will be grief for the next few months. Everything. Laughter and tears. Solitude and the need for company. Eating and fasting. And many unusual stories and memories, including animal stories."

After all, from the Egyptians with their animal-headed deities to Native American traditions with their vivid animal totems so linked to the human soul, to the lion of St. Mark and the eagle of St. John, animals have opened the door for many of us onto experiences of spirit, wonder, and yes, grief. Not only religious images bring animals to our minds during grief but also simpler, more homespun pictures kept in our hearts, like memories of the unconditional love of a lapping puppy or the soothing beauty of a cat stretching languorously in a square of sunlight.

As I contemplate aspects of grief and loss, I also remember this: We too are animals.

grief

and relief

When my grandfather Nazzareno died, he was very old, in his mid-nineties. I was thirty, living in California, and knew I was fortunate indeed to have known and loved him for so long, and to have been loved by him.

Nazzareno was my father's father, and my father, who adored him, was in anguish watching him suffer. The doctor had taught my mother to give my grandfather shots to relieve his pain, which was considerable. My father was glad she had learned that skill, since he was simply unable to do it. My grandfather had cried out for his mother, my mother told me one day. Another time, he cried out in dialect, "Iacmet, come take me." No one in the family had ever heard that word before, but we decided it must have been some Emilian mountain word for what in English is sometimes called the Grim Reaper.

When my grandfather finally died, my mother called to tell me. I wailed, and then I settled down to begin to figure out how to get back to Detroit for his funeral. When I saw his body laid out at the funeral home, I wailed again. Loudly. My mother came to me and said, "Mark, it has been a relief to us that he died. He was in such pain. It was hard to watch. We felt for him so much. You don't have to cry so much. It's okay."

I said to her, "Ma, I know that you have cared for him while I have been away, and I thank you for that. I understand your relief. But please realize that I am not crying about the man who just died. I am grieving for the man who used to hold me on his shoulder when I was two years old, the only person in the family who could get me to sleep, the man who took walks with me every day to see the trains I loved, the man who taught me how to listen to the slight hiss the wine makes in the barrel when it is ready to bottle, the man who took me to Palmer Park on the bus to pick pounds of mushrooms with him. That's who I am grieving."

Over the years, I too have felt relieved when certain people have died. My friend John Zimarowski, one of the first people I knew who died of AIDS, had lost his sense of self and could no longer recognize anyone. And he was clearly suffering pain. I was not only devastated when he died but also relieved. Another friend was suffering so much that he asked me to help him die, which

I found I could not do. When my friend Flip had lost most of his sense of self due to early-onset Alzheimer's disease and had to wear a helmet because he stumbled around banging his head against the wall, his wife and I prayed that his suffering might end soon.

Relief is a significant chapter in the scrolls of grief. We need not feel ashamed or guilty about our sense of relief that accompanies the death of someone who has suffered. Yet as the story of my grandfather illustrates, people will experience relief from different vantage points. For my mother, who had witnessed his suffering, the relief was palpable. For me, who had not, the relief was more intellectual, something my head understood, certainly, but which my heart could not.

The idea of relief can make sense even when the person who died did not suffer terrible physical pain at the end. Many decades ago I met a woman whose father had sexually abused her from age six to age thirteen. This cruelly twisted her life in many ways. She got help, however, and over a seven-year period restored her life to a remarkably beautiful balance. But it meant cutting herself off from her family and creating another entirely new and healthy family. When she got news of her father's death, she felt a sense of relief as well as sadness. She knew that his drinking had paved the way for his violence, and that he had finally died because of complications due to the alcohol. He had not contacted her since she left home to save herself, and she had kept up with his life through her siblings. They knew he had abused her, and they were glad that she had the strength to move away from this sad and tragic man. Her relief at his death served to cap the healing she had begun by leaving her family.

Sometimes relief comes even at the death of someone truly beloved. When my mother's mother, Anna, died after more than eleven years in a home for people with Alzheimer's disease, the relief was very real. My mother had cared for my grandmother at home for a long time, too long in my estimation. This was because a woman, whom I did not know, had responded to my mother's sigh about how much it took out of her to care for someone who couldn't speak or walk anymore. "Oh, Lisa," the woman said, "you're not going to put your mother in a home, are you?" My mother was shamed into doing the kind of nursing for which she had never been trained. Finally, my sister Lynne and I prevailed, and our grandmother was moved to a place that specialized in the care of Alzheimer's patients and was well taken care of there. For the entire time she was there, my grandmother didn't know who she herself was, let alone my mother or me or the staff. Grief at her mother's slow-motion loss while she was still alive ("She has the heart of a twenty-five year old," one doctor surprisingly affirmed) dominated my mother's inner life for a long time. But day by day, the heft of shame placed on her heart lifted. Grandma Anna's death, as my mother said when she called to tell me that she had finally died, was "a blessing," her loss "a gift."

As it had been with my beloved grandfather Nazzareno twenty-three years before.

grief

and life

Although the deaths of those I love have shaped much of my thinking about grief, I am quite aware that loss, as Siddhartha, the Buddha, pointed out millennia ago, is with all of us every day in the flow of our lives.

Grief arises when I lose touch with a friend with whom I used to be close. "We've grown apart" is the common explanation for such events, but that does not mean I do not grieve. Although I cultivate friendships, sometimes they end anyway. We feel grief when leaving a job after years, or even a few weeks, if we liked the work but the new owners downsized us.

We experience grief when a shop or theater we have patronized for twenty years finally closes. We experience grief when something precious disappears: photos destroyed in a house fire or a bicycle stolen. A painting of mine was stolen once from an exhibit at my university's gallery, and I grieved the loss. The grief I felt then was not on a par with the grief I felt when Laszlo Toth took a hammer to Michelangelo's *Pieta* or when a thief tucked Edvard Munch's *The Scream* underarm and walked off. But it was grief.

I have grieved at the end of a job, even if I resigned for good reasons. I have grieved when I have moved. I grieved when I moved away from a congregation I loved for eighteen years. I have grieved when friendships that once flashed brightly simply faded away, our lives taking us in divergent directions. I grieved when my beloved supervisor retired. I grieved when my internship ended. I grieved when a cherished minister moved to another congregation. I grieved when two colleagues I cared for were removed from fellowship because of inappropriate sexual conduct. I grieve every day as I prepare to retire from my present beloved congregation. I grieve when a person known to most everyone from screen or stage—Robin Williams comes to mind—dies.

I was born and raised in Detroit, as of this writing one of the sadder places on earth. Plant life has grown over the block where my grandmother Carmelina lived, curbs eaten by weeds, houses burned to the ground, all save five. I grieve every time I drive through the city on my way to visit my sister, who has moved far to the north, far away from the objective misery.

I grieved when a seriously disturbed person in the first congregation I served focused her projections on me and wrote vile letters to me daily for more than a year. I felt as though I was walking on eggshells every time I went to the mailbox or opened my door (she had threatened to kill me, but this was long enough ago that no laws were on the books for such harassment). I had lost my sense of daily well-being entirely and grieved for that equanimity, and I wondered if ministry was indeed possible for me. I worked with a brilliant therapist who helped me to strategize a conclusion to this nightmare, but to this day, if I see someone who resembles her, I flinch and shut down, even though she herself is long gone.

We feel grief when we lose some aspect of our health: loss of motion due to arthritis, loss of a diet of familiar foods because of an allergy that develops, loss of breast or limb or eyesight or hearing. When the cardiologist told me I had a permanent heart condition due, he theorized, to some virus, I grieved the loss of life without daily pills and regular echocardiograms. When a floater appeared in my eye, large and web-like, I grieved the loss of unimpaired peripheral vision.

In this age when Alzheimer's disease still afflicts, one can experience loss of self too. My dear friend Flip suffered the difficulties of early-onset Alzheimer's, and died at age fifty-eight. But long before that he had lost his memory, and his sense of self, which had been built on the foundations of that memory.

Even acquaintances who disappear from our lives elicit grief. I used to compose my Sunday service materials, longhand, at a cafe in Oakland, a bright place with large windows and good coffee. Since I worked there often, I got to know Mike, the guy most often behind the counter when I went. He would see me turning the pages of a book, looking for a reading, and sometimes he would come over to my table on his break and ask about what I was doing. I asked him about his life too. For more than a year, we chatted and talked about philosophy, relationships, even poetry. It was a delightful, reliable part of my life that I enjoyed. We never visited together outside the café, but we liked each other immensely.

One day he told me he was taking a trip to Germany, a place he had wanted to visit for a long time. He was going to be gone for more than a month, maybe two. He said he wanted to write me, and I gladly gave him my address. He told me he would send me a permanent mailing address from Europe where I could contact him.

He did. He sent me a beautiful letter. I wrote him back immediately. Two months later, the letter came back unopened. No such person at that address anymore. I never saw him or heard from him again. No clear finality, just suspension of presence. Eventually I gave in and grieved his loss in the usual manner. It wasn't dramatic as when I lost my good friend John Zimarowski to death, but it was grief nevertheless.

Becoming aware of the smaller or denied griefs in our lives can help us let go of the invisible, and often larger spiritual aches in our tender hearts that sometimes keep us from moving forward for reasons we have not yet named.

Grief holds hands with life. Life holds hands with grief.

grief

and philosophy

Sometimes, as I age and watch people coming and going, living and dying, and the generations rising and falling, as I watch what was once familiar and understandable fade or get replaced by something new and complex, I say this: "Growing older is compulsory Buddhism." What I mean is that as I understand it, Siddhartha Gautama saw pretty much all life, and creation itself, as nothing but loss and change, arrival and departure, beginnings and endings. Nothing is permanent.

Call it a religious proclamation or call it philosophy, it seems pretty true to me, and I find myself holding on less tightly to things—and even people—as I grow older.

Some time ago, an acquaintance named Joe, who had been born in Hong Kong, told me a story about the Chinese philosopher Zhuangzi, who lived in the third century BCE. Joe and I had been talking philosophically about our attitudes toward death, and he told me this story to illustrate his perspective on the matter. I was so intrigued by the story that I wrote down some of the details.

After a long and happy marriage, Zhuangzi's wife died. When he found out, Zhuangzi's friend Hui Shi came by to pay his respects. I am not sure what he expected to find, but Hui Shi was certainly put out by what he did find. There was Zhuangzi, holding an upside-down pan between his knees as if it were a drum. He was thumping his fingers on the pan and singing loudly to the wild beat.

"Zhuangzi, what *are* you doing? You lived with your wife happily for decades. She was a good mother to your children, and you aged together gracefully." Hui Shi was so shocked, in fact, that he went on berating his friend. "It's bad enough that you aren't weeping and crying out in grief right now. But I think you have gone entirely too far by all this drumming and singing."

"Do not trouble me so!" Zhuangzi said. "Look, when she first died, do you really think I wasn't feeling the loss as deeply as possible? Do you really think I didn't weep? But then I looked back to the time before she was born, when she was not here, had no body or vital life. And something happened. As it always does. First, out of the whirl of time, something changed and vital life appeared on earth. Then that vital life took forms until it took on her form; with changes in form, her life began. Now there is another change in this world, a change that brings death. Hui Shi, how is this different from the procession of the four seasons of spring and fall, winter and summer? I saw her there in her large room, where she had fallen into the sleep of death. I entered the room and I sobbed and wailed. But even as I wailed, I began to think about the world we both shared, the seasons, the spinning sky. And I realized that my actions showed I hadn't understood how things really are, and so I stopped, and now I do what brings me pleasure still, no matter the season, and that is, as you can see, drumming and singing."

The Hebrew wisdom literature in the scriptures also philosophizes about death, rather plainly. Here is my translation of two passages from the scroll of Qoheleth, also called Ecclesiastes:

So, go on, and eat your bread with gladness, and down your wine with a joyous heart, for already, G-d has blessed what you are doing. Always wear your best clothes, and keep yourself well-groomed. Live out your life fully with the one you love, all the days of your allotted span of life here under the sun, fleeting as they are. For that is your fortune here on the earth: to live and work hard. Whatever task is at hand, do it with the full force of your strength, because I tell you, in the grave, where we're all headed, there is no doing things, no thinking of thoughts, no understanding and certainly, no wisdom.

The living know they are mortal. The dead know nothing at all. They will receive no awards, and they will soon be forgotten.

This is not the heaven many people seem to think is found in Western scriptures. Of course, even that heaven is not heaven, especially the pop heaven of the cartoons and jokes, with St. Peter at his desk; it's not the rather capitalistic heaven of those who mine the Revelation of John for a philosophy of life beyond death that simply is not there: jeweled gates, golden streets. When Matthew's Jesus uses the phrase kingdom of heaven (or empire of heaven, or realm of heaven) there is no evidence he was even talking about personal survival after death. He was describing the dominion of the divine here on earth—in a mustard seed, in a field with a buried treasure, in a beautiful pearl, in a wedding feast, in a fig tree, in a loaf of bread. An earthy philosophy indeed.

What the historic son of Mary thought about death remains elusive, despite the claims of those who, in their worship of the idol I call Certainty, seem rather sure that they know.

Some philosophers have been clearer. Aristotle seems to have suggested that death was something fearful, whereas Epicurus thought the exact opposite. Does this mean Aristotle wept when he lost a friend and Epicurus went around dry-eyed? Aristotle thought that weeping was a healthful and excellent way to work through emotions. Epicurus may have wept for the foolish situation of the world outside his garden, but he was clear that grief, even for a friend who died, should not "beat you up." Yet, I have to imagine that even Epicurus, when he lost a friend (and friendship for him was of inestimable value), would have acknowledged that a singular member of the world who had helped Epicurus *be* Epicurus was significant, whether he wept or not.

Søren Kierkegaard advised "reflective grief," meaning a grief that invites philosophical observation, and also suggested that those of different ages grieve differently, and that we might unjustly accuse other generations of grieving too much or too little. No doubt culture plays a role in expressions of grief too. That my rather reserved grandfather threw himself into the open coffin of his dead brother, crying in Italian, "Goodbye, my brother," might strike others as over the top, but in my culture, such displays, especially in the older generation, are neither surprising nor prone to critique from others who share that culture.

Of course, not all philosophy about loss and grief comes from the pens (or keyboards) of the famous. Nor is it always couched in the more abstract language often favored by philosophers, like Edmund Husserl, for example. After my father's parents died, he wept, for he loved them very much. But after a time his grief took the form of a story. He would speak of his parents sitting around a table with their pre-deceased friends, playing the card game pinochle "forever." Was this my father's idea of heaven? No, he made clear to me that, though loyal to Sunday mass at the local Roman Catholic parish, he, like his father, Nazzareno, believed in no such thing. "When you die, you die," he would say to me quite plainly.

But the pleasure my grandparents took in playing cards with their friends was how my father wanted to remember them. He would smile as he told this story. He didn't say it represented his philosophy or pretend it reflected some sort of theology. It was simply the way his grief grew more reflective with time. Would Epicurus have lectured him on being more restrained in his imaginative way of seeing things? Perhaps.

I just know that the tears, and all the emotions they indicate, join with my idea of compulsory Buddhism to allow me to welcome grief fully into my life, but not become totally overwhelmed by it.

grief

and moving

Over the years I have talked with people who call themselves army brats, which means that they grew up in military families and relocated around the country as often as once per year. A woman in the church I served in California claimed such a history for herself, and when I was about to move to Ohio, she offered to help me pack. I have to say, she taught me the meaning of the phrase "practice makes perfect." She packed so efficiently and so well that it was like watching a Japanese tea ceremony—no wasted motion. When I arrived in Columbus, not one glass had broken, not one dish cracked.

I don't know if the frequency of moves endured by so-called army brats inured them to what I went through, but moving to Ohio after a quarter century in California introduced me to a different kind of grief. My friends were not dying, but I knew I was going to mostly relate to them by phone from that time on. I couldn't just drop in on Doug for a conversation and some ice cream or attend seder with Richard's family by simply crossing the Bay Bridge. The familiarity of the Oakland streets was going to be replaced by the unfamiliarity of Columbus streets. The circle of friends who gathered at my place on holidays for family meals would not be gathering in Ohio. I would find no familiar doctor's face, greengrocer, or auto mechanic without searching diligently and taking some time to get to know them. Traffic laws would be different, the history of the community would be different, and the ethnic mix would be different. *Different* hardly means *bad* to me, but negotiating that many differences all at once because I was moving across the country was downright overwhelming.

In the last months before packing, I found myself saying goodbye, sometimes literally, to every familiar palm tree, Victorian gable, rosemary hedge, and hill I could see. I walked the Taraval beach at sunset and said goodbye to the sand dollars on the pink shore, nodded goodbye to Le Cheval, my favorite Vietnamese restaurant, and walked the full length of Market Street—the street I and thirty thousand others, holding candles, had processed down on the evening of the day Harvey Milk was assassinated—saying goodbye to every block along the way. My inner life, being so interwoven with my exterior life, my experiences of my environment, and my circles of love and loss, would never be the same again. Which meant *I* would never be the same again. I hoped to grow and deepen, certainly, but I knew the loss of place and context was going to change me no matter what.

Moving from state to state is one form of moving. But I have moved from other contexts in my life as well, and all of them, I now know, engaged aspects of grief: grief as relief, when I stopped forging leaf springs for trucks in a factory that worked me so hard I thought I had never worked before. Grief as deep sorrow, when I left my amazing colleagues at Hawthorn Center in Northville, Michigan, where we worked with disturbed children in residential treatment.

I have wrestled with loss of health too, a move from life without medication to life with daily medication until my last day, once my heart issue was discovered. It seems like a small thing, since the heart problem I have doesn't have much exterior effect. Nevertheless, it's a real change that affects my self-awareness in new ways.

I don't know how those who move from state to state on a yearly basis manage to cope with such drastic changes and adjustments, always saying hello and good-bye, but I have met many who have nurtured strength of spirit because of it. Maybe because I have moved only twice in my life, the grief I have experienced with a move felt remarkably powerful. But as with other grief I've experienced, my metaphoric heart has found more ways to be vulnerable to the world than I had ever before imagined.

grief

and anger

A beloved friend called and told me that his father had died just a few weeks back while I was out of town. I expressed my condolences and suggested we get together to talk.

We went to Mouton, a small, late-night place in Columbus with perfect noshes, great wines, and high stools lining the large windows, where we could speak to each other without being drowned out by the avid conversations behind us.

My friend told me about his father, whom he loved. We spoke of their attempts to say goodbye to each other in the ways that were possible to each of them. And we talked of his grieving. My friend, who had experienced a lot of heartache recently with the end of a five-year, much-treasured relationship with a woman overseas, was pretty articulate. Everyday routines that brought out his faithfulness—early rising, brisk exercise—suddenly seemed irrelevant to him. His sleep schedule was unpredictable. And he found that anger was always simmering nearby.

Pique. Easy aggravation. None of this was directed toward his father, whom he deeply cared about. The anger surfaced, he told me, mostly at work. Snapping. Fuming. But even at home, when little things went wrong, like dropping something.

My friend ordinarily is a man of quiet strength, with a warm and easy laugh and visible groundedness. But as we sat on those stools and conversed, it became clear to me that he was saturated with grief. I suggested to him that anger and crankiness is one form grief takes for many of us, and that I too had been impatient, quick to curse and grind my teeth in the months after my brother had died. I suggested to him, and to myself, that it might take some time for each of us to find our native equilibrium again, our deeper joy and appreciation, our longer contentment with our routines, our work, and our own centered inner lives.

I remembered that not all grief-anger rises without a personal focus. I dearly loved a colleague, a true friend with whom I frequently spoke. He lived two states to the north of me, and we mostly saw each other at conferences. The last time I saw him we were at one of those conferences, in the Canadian Rockies, and we joined another beloved friend to row across Lake Louise on the most perfect powder-blue day any of the three of us could remember. The cracking ice on the steep mountains that nested the lake, the lap of the waves on the side of the boat, the laughter and poignancy of three friends sharing their deep hopes, the bright ligaments of afternoon light connecting us heart to heart, deep to deep, and the three of us to sky and mountain and water were almost too dazzling. That day carried me forward in peace and gratitude for many months. Later that fall my friend called me (sometimes daily), to talk about his doubts. His doubts about his work, his life, his religious sensibility, his happiness. He told me he was seeing a professional and taking a certain medication to help him with his downward spiral. He had a medical background and spoke with confidence about his capacity to find himself again spiritually. He even broached the subject of entering a monastery, where he imagined a different life for himself and a different religious practice that he hoped would embrace him with a reliable and ancient beauty.

In November of that same year, I returned from work one day to hear a message on my answering machine. "I'm sorry about your friend. Call me." Who? What? Another message. Another voice. "I'm sorry about your friend. Call me." No answer at either number. Finally, I called the seminary and asked to talk with my favorite professor. Did he know anything?

He did. My friend had taken his own life. I immediately started to cry. But in a flash, my tears disappeared and a gorge of rage rose up inside me. I shook my fist at heaven and cursed my friend. "How dare you take your own life! Don't you know how loved you were? People told you that all the time. They never held back. We *all* loved you."

I was shaking with rage for a good long time.

According to psychotherapist and teacher David Richo, in his 2008 book *When the Past Is Present*, grief is composed of three feelings: sadness that something was lost, anger that it was taken away, and fear that it will never be replaced. This suggests that anger in some form or another might accompany almost any grieving process. I would certainly agree. But my anger at my friend taking his own life was of a decidedly different order. His loss shook me in a new and frightening way.

Yet, as the day wore on, I remembered that I had often told my friend how many people told *me* how much they loved *him*. "I know that," he used to say to me, "but somehow it never gets past my skin."

I began to realize that my anger was based on my overgenerous expectation that love can heal everything. Sometimes, I now admit, even love is not enough. And so my anger ebbed, to be replaced by a more tender sorrow and a rather redeeming understanding.

Years later, when I watched the controversial film *Shortbus*, I revisited my sorrow and set it in a larger context. In the story, another well-loved man, James, expresses exactly the same words as my friend had. After James tries to take his own life, the man who saves him from drowning says to him, "You have so much. Jamie loves you." Then James looks at him and says, "I see it all around me, but it stops at my skin. I can't let it inside. It's always been like that." I sat in the movie theater for a while, my eyes wet with hot tears.

The tears I wept at the movie theater were for my friend who had died a decade before, but this time they were not mixed with anger. I reminded myself never to discount any love that flows from me or toward me. It can't save everything, but it sure helps at the time of grief.

Sometimes the anger associated with grief has a slightly different edge to it. When Stewart, a member of the congregation in San Francisco, told me he wanted to study for the ministry, I spoke with him many times, asking all the hard questions. After getting to know what a remarkable man he was, I wrote avid letters of support to the Pacific School of Religion, to which he had applied. He got in, and we often talked with excitement about what he was learning. Stewart was filled with an overbrimming spirit; his clear blue eyes radiated excitement about life, love, and knowledge.

After a few months I got word that a drunk driver had hit and killed Stewart, twenty-seven years old, as he stood on a street corner not far from the church, waiting to cross. Stewart was the only child of his parents, adopted, loved fiercely, and I sympathized with their impossible grief as I keened my own.

But then an anger in me, with a ferocity I had never known, gripped my throat. I wanted to find the man who killed Stewart in his drunken stupor and do something terrible to him. When I found out later that his killer had received three driving under the influence citations and was driving without a license, I went ballistic. I joined the organization Mothers Against Drunk Driving and gave furious speeches at rallies. I wrote letters to judges and to the editors of great newspapers, and I found myself easily irritable for many months.

My anger that Stewart was "taken away" is one kind of anger, according to Richo, one associated with the course of grief. My anger at the drunk driver was sparked by that grief, to be sure, but deep down it sprang from more of a social, not a personal source. Moreover, the personal anger at losing Stewart was attached at the hip to other aspects of grief: sorrow, memory, depression, and even gratitude—gratitude that I had been fortunate enough to bear witness, even for that short time, to Stewart's overflowing love of life.

Sitting there that evening at Mouton I told my friend he would live with his anger for a while. Everything in life seems smaller than the death of a parent, and quick irritation with lesser things is testimony to that. I told him the anger would lessen with time and be replaced by tenderness, sorrow, and even gratitude. All forms of that powerful, if not all powerful, grace: love.

grief
and astonishment

More often than you might imagine, folks come up to me after I have offered a eulogy for another parishioner and say, "I wish we could hear the eulogies you give *before* someone dies, and not just afterward. I wish I had known all those things about her so that I could have talked with her about them. She never told me she was an aspiring flute player. I am too. I thought I knew her pretty well, but I guess I didn't. There is so much we don't know about each other."

True. And I understand the sentiment.

Over and over again while preparing a memorial, I have been astonished by how rich human lives are, and sometimes how tragic.

When I look out on Sunday from the pulpit, the faces of the people whose friends or family I have buried shine with stories I now know.

But a more basic astonishment surfaces when I grieve, and that is the mystery of life and death itself. That we are here. At all. That all lives are mortal. That every single life born in the nineteenth century is gone now, and in a hundred years, so may all life on earth right now be gone. Sometimes as I walk to my car in the oddly yellow light that illuminates my building's garage, I find myself astonished by that light, by the three dimensionality and apparent solidity of everything around me. Oh, I accept what the physicists tell me, namely, that we are mostly made of up empty space. But it looks so permanent. "It's all here!" I find myself saying over and over. "Everything is!"

Astonishing.

I marvel that there are people in Malaysia and Nunavat and in the cities of Perm or Valparaiso I will never know, yet whose lives are as important to them as mine is to me. And they grieve in the manners outlined by culture and family systems when someone they love closes her eyes for the last time.

I remember the first time I witnessed the death of a fellow human being. He had been unconscious for weeks, but suddenly, astonishingly, he opened his eyes, looked at his wife and then at me. He lifted himself up on his bone-like arms, spoke his last tender love to his wide-eyed wife, spoke his goodbye to me, and said to us both, "I'm going now, goodbye." Then he lay down, stopped breathing, and grew quiet.

For weeks afterward, all I could think about was that transition, from life to stillness. His surprising voice announcing that he was going just then echoed in my head for weeks, as if my skull had become a hollow cave with nothing else but that goodbye resounding within.

Astonishment and grief were welded together on that day for me.

When I was walking through City Lights bookstore in San Francisco one day I chanced upon a book by the powerful poet Fernando Pessoa titled *Always Astonished*.

"I'll say!" I said out loud, as if speaking to Pessoa himself on the shelf. The friend who was with me then asked, "What does *that* mean?" So I told her the story I have just told you, but in richer detail, and when I was through she said, "Ah. I see. You know, come to think of it, I am too. Always astonished about the mystery that we live at all and all are mortal."

To which I simply said, "Amen."

grief

and gratitude

My mother died two days before Thanksgiving in 2011. On that day I was visiting my friend Mike in Cincinnati, and both of us were planning to shop at Jungle Jim's, the large food store there; I, in particular, for the Thanksgiving dinner for ten I was cooking for and hosting. It was raining hard that day. As we got out of the car to go into the store, my sister called to tell me that our mother had just died.

Right there in the dark, driving rain of late November, I wailed loudly and told my sister I would call her back. Michael held me for a moment, and then, sensibly, he led me out of the rain. He held me again inside the store as I sobbed. When I called my sister back, I learned she had already made arrangements with the priest for the requiem, which would be Saturday. So I told her that I would still host my Thanksgiving dinner in Columbus and then go up to Detroit later in the day so that I could offer a eulogy on Friday at the funeral home.

It happened as we had decided. My guests all arrived earlier than usual. We toasted my mother, enjoyed our day, and then at two o'clock I told them I needed to leave to go up north. My dear friend John organized the cleanup, and they put my place back in order before they left. Me, I climbed into my car for a four-hour drive up Highway 23 through the orange afternoon sunlight to the northern suburbs of Detroit.

As I drove, I played a CD of Karl Jenkins's *Stabat Mater*. "Stood the mournful mother weeping" runs the text, speaking of Mary at the foot of the cross. The melody of Jenkins's version of this medieval poem is not particularly sad, but rather thoughtful, reflective—even hopeful. And very beautiful.

As the music played and I drove through the afternoon light, I was overwhelmed by a sense of joy, a sense of deep gratitude that Elisa had been my mother, that our conversations in recent years had been so redemptive and transformative, that she had revealed so much of her heart to me toward the end. Images of her life, images of her face raced across the screen of sunlight. I felt in my bones and tingling on the surface of my skin a deep, deep gratitude, a joyous sense of satisfaction that my life had been so blessed.

A negative voice inside me said, "You are driving up to deliver the eulogy at your mother's funeral, and you are spilling over in joy and thanks?" I immediately silenced the voice by answering, "This too is grieving. Overwhelming gratitude."

I remembered that I had felt this way for a while after my best friend, Stephen, had died. At a collegial gathering in Hot Springs, Arkansas, just a few weeks after his memorial rituals, I was talking with a dear colleague, Meg Riley, about Stephen. As we talked, I found a sense of increasing joy and gratitude moving through my body, a brightness that I had not felt in a long time. Yes, Stephen had died at age forty—very young, too soon, and all that—but what a life he lived, and how wondrous and remarkable was our long friendship. How much I learned from him, how tenderly and boisterously we related to each other. I was surprised then, too. Where was my sorrow, my sobbing? Where had the desolation gone?

I realized then how those feelings were still there, but not as important or as dazzling as the gratitude.

Of course, it's fair to say that I deeply loved both my mother and Stephen. My grief for them was surely magnified by that depth of feeling.

But I do remind those who come to me to talk about their grieving experiences not to be surprised if this feeling of gratitude wells up in them. Sometimes I will even say to folks who have lost someone beloved that "everything is grief for a while: tears and laughter both, depression and joy, relief and crankiness, desolation and fresh openings into life."

Grief, I've come to see, is not a single feeling in and of itself but a whole symphony of feelings, some seemingly deeply dissonant from each other. But then, great symphonies often grow richer with the incorporation of dissonance so that the remarkable resolution at the conclusion seems all the more a gift.

grief

and guilt

When I told my friend Doug that I was working on a chapter called "Grief and Guilt" and how quickly I thought I could finish writing it, he was surprised.

"Guilt? Wouldn't that take weeks? Months?" He said it with a grin, but of course, his question makes sense. Guilt is a ponderous and sharp feeling in many lives, and it has so many dimensions that months, even years spent exploring it would hardly unfold its power.

I often hear folks with a religious upbringing debate who grew up feeling the most guilt. Religion certainly can play a role in how people feel guilt. But I confess to being surprised that the word *guilt* itself, as in the feeling of guilt, is not found any place in either the Jewish or the Christian testaments. Not once. The few times the English word can be found in more antique translations, it refers only to the kind of "guilty" that courts speak about, which is not a feeling so much as a legal category.

I am convinced that families of origin, cultural and ethnic patterns, and characterological realities play a far greater role in how much guilt we feel than does religion. I certainly have known folks raised without religion of any kind—including the "shopping mall spirituality" created by the cultus of consumerism—who have struggled with guilt as much as anyone raised in a particular denomination of religion, Western or Eastern.

Guilt can often be found within the folds of grief. It usually takes the form of self-recrimination:

"I didn't visit her enough."

"I didn't say goodbye in time."

"I went to a wedding and my mother died while I was having fun there."

"I never told him the truth about the affair I had."

"I put too much trust in medicine. I should have questioned everything on my father's behalf."

"I questioned the doctors too much. I was irritable and a pest. I feel so bad about how I behaved."

"I feel guilty that I kept on thinking about my inheritance."

"I feel guilty that I never got past my brother's perpetual and self-righteous preaching, and didn't feel the least bit sad when he finally died. I was glad in fact to never have to hear one of his rants ever again."

"I feel terrible that I cursed God when my son died. I hope he can forgive me. But I really hated God with a passion for a while, and feel terrible about that."

"She wouldn't have died if I had prayed more fervently."

Variations on all these themes have run through conversations I've had with fellow grievers, and I've certainly struggled with aspects of guilt myself, especially wondering if I might have taken more time off from work to be with dying friends; particularly the ones rejected by their families.

But guilt is a feeling, not a rational judgment. In the AIDS days in the San Francisco Bay Area, if I had taken time off work to spend more time with all my friends and acquaintances who were dying, I wouldn't have been able to work at all. Nor have a moment to myself. The fact is, all of us who went through that era, in the Bay Area or any place else, did a lot and more, gladly giving of our time for those we loved. But we are finite beings, with physical and temporal and even emotional limits, and trying to deny that remains foolish.

Guilt may be a symbol of other feelings too—inadequacy, exhaustion, resentment—that we simply don't wish to admit to ourselves.

But guilt has another association, a social one. The curse "You are a bleeding-heart liberal," still a mainstay of so-called talk radio here in the United States, means that you spend too much time feeling guilty about the evils of the world and are wasting your time confronting them. You are letting your feelings of compassion rather than "common sense" govern your actions.

You hear that curse, and sarcastic variations of it, especially when radio and television pundits defend their preachments against the power and dignity of women, or deny that race has meaning anymore, or insist that sexual minorities are directly responsible for both hurricanes and the crucifixion of Christ, or put down the natives of this land with a snicker and lob innuendos at their singing, religion, clothing, or difficult history. I guess only "bleeding-heart liberals" are moved by such things.

Often, when these social issues are raised, especially about racial and native issues, I hear protests: "I wasn't responsible. My ancestors were not here then. Don't look at me."

This is why I am so moved by the writings of Axel Gehrmann, a Unitarian Universalist minister in Illinois who was born and raised in Germany. He reports that his generation, who had nothing at all to do with Auschwitz, nevertheless refused to hide out on the other side of guilt by denying responsibility. Inspired by *Our Inability to Grieve*, a book written by two psychologists, Axel's generation began to grieve for what happened, even though they had not participated in the murders of so many. His generation understands that systemic cultural histories led to the Shoah, the so-called Holocaust, and that just because Auschwitz is no longer a death camp does not mean that the cultural history behind the creation of Auschwitz evaporated.

Working in small groups, the younger generations engaged with older generations of Germans who *had* been caught up in the war, struggling with their values in the violent turmoil of the age. Little by little, things changed. They faced guilt square on. They began grieving for a terrible time in German history. They admitted responsibility and wrestled with shame. Thus Germany entered a process that our North American nations have resisted for two hundred years, regarding what the colonialists did to the natives of this land and for the institution of chattel slavery. Our inability to grieve for the actions of our ancestors has led to the present state of affairs, in which a small percentage own and run nearly everything, and feel entitled to do so, while the vast majority increasingly lose their place at the "welcome table." The idea that some human beings simply have the right to overlook others has now become the water in which we swim. Protesting against this reality will have little effect unless we grieve and mourn for the mess we have made, not personally but culturally. Community grief. Grief as a whole nation.

Doug was right. If I addressed the subject of grief and guilt fully, I would write for months. But it's important to mention the social aspect of grief as well as the personal, and dwell less on the supposed religious origins of grief and instead dwell on the deep social impact of our inability to grieve. The path to this grief is a spiritual one. It will enable our spirit, our breath, to once again breathe without constraint. Grieving can even address the perverse claustrophobia named "It's the way it is and has been; nothing can be done."

This life has many spiritual paths, many ways to go deeper and to rise from the shallows. Many ways to live our lives with power and without the blinders of shame or denial. But of all the spiritual paths, grieving is basic and, in many ways, the foundation of all the rest.

May the younger generations in North America show the way as they did in Germany. It's worth hoping for. It's worth it for all of us to join them and to finally, finally grow up and claim the gift of our humanity.

grief

and culture

My young friend Devere put the liveliness in life. I can never think of him without a smile coming to my face. Devere and I initially connected over art; he did drawings and so did I. Other than that, our differences were obvious—me, more than halfway through life; he, still in his twenties. Me, in a vocation I love; he, still figuring it all out. Me, an Italian American raised in a white neighborhood in northern Detroit just shy of the first suburb; he, born into what Clevelanders call the "ghetto." "Nice Italian word, *ghetto*," I used to joke with him. "That means we're cousins!" he said, with his infectious laugh.

One day, his housing opportunities unexpectedly collapsed, so I invited him to live in my guest room temporarily. He ended up staying, to my joy, almost two years. During those years, I have never laughed so much in my life. He could find the humor in everything, and he was brilliant at lifting it up. "Stop it!" I used to protest, as I convulsed in laughter. "You want me to develop abs or something?" He was not only hilarious, but he pitched in to help make the place his home too: He cleaned and did laundry and helped me take care of the loft. It would be glowing when I came back from professional or personal trips. He was the perfect housemate.

Some folks raised their eyebrows and said that they thought of us as "unlikely" friends. But, foolish them, ours grew into a deep and sustaining friendship. Besides laughing, we shared our hearts and questions and disappointments with each other. At holiday meals, everyone else there found Devere as marvelous as I did. He enjoyed my friends and my son, Tony. Folks who met him at church commented on what a delight he was in conversation. I came to know his wonderful mother, Ladosha, who visited us frequently. Devere revered his grandmother like I revered my grandmother Carmalina, and he always wanted me to meet her up in Cleveland. With my schedule conflicting with his, we never made it.

He worked at a café, to the delight of everyone there, gliding among the clientele with his effervescent joy.

But, sadly, Devere seroconverted and faced the impact of HIV at age twenty-five. He resisted treatment at first. He lived in denial for a while, as many do. I used to offer to go with him to the doctor, but at the last minute he always backed out. Ladosha and I worried. Eventually, his mother moved him down to Atlanta where there was a particular treatment plan she thought would be best for him.

But sadly, even with that magnificent effort, it wasn't long before he died. My wailing, as you can certainly imagine, went on for days. But Ladosha offered me the privilege of conducting his memorial service. It took place in the common room of his high school in suburban Cleveland, where his mother had moved when he was an older child so that he might benefit from the better schools that our racialized society often reserves for people mostly of European ancestry.

Devere was not a church goer. He was not raised with institutional religion, though he was surrounded by many Pentecostal relatives. And so, when I got to Cleveland on a suitably cold and rainy day, I was not the only leader in the service.

I offered my eulogy, but others spoke of his relationship to Christ, which at first baffled me. After some time, I remembered what I had learned over the years about the relationship between religion and culture. Religious belief and cultural expectations are not always the same thing. Religious belief is always expressed through the lens of the community's cultural expectations. For many people there, some reference to a relationship to Christ identified the free-form ritual of that hour *as* a funeral. Not the Mary J. Blige music, nor my loving words about his glowing, brief life, but that.

I began to think about the various cultural differences I had encountered around the nation. Where I grew up, in the industrial and rather Catholic Midwest, the main cultural expression of community grief was not so much the requiem at the church, but the three-day wake at the funeral home. People gathered there to express official condolences to the grievers and to tell stories, do business, gossip a bit. It was a portable town square. In some funeral homes that primarily served particular ethnic groups, you might hear the sound of professional mourners making quite a scene, or you might see icons of special saints or holy figures.

Yet when I moved to California, quite a few people were openly shocked by the idea of a body visible in a casket. One fellow even said to me, "What a barbaric custom! People actually do that?" Yet, that is the culture that made sense to me. It seemed more visceral to me than the quick removal of the body, never to be seen again. I often wanted to be with the dead body of a congregant while it was still in the hospital awaiting transportation to a mortuary. It helped me to grieve, to make the death real for my whole person, not just my mind. "But why?" people would ask. "That is not them anymore. Remember them as they were when they were younger or glowing with health."

"I know, and I do," I often retorted, "but this is my culture, and it helps me with my grief, and does not distort it in any way."

When I have conducted memorials, I can count on many people in attendance not being part of my religious circles. Some come from other religious or cultural communities far removed from my own. Others have never been part of a religious organization, and still others believe that all memorials must be just like the ones they knew growing up—which often scared them with threats of hell at the end, such threats being part of the close of such services. Some have thoroughly rejected religion in all of its forms, and are clearly uncomfortable sitting in a building with religious associations, despite their very real love for the person who has died. I identify all this variety plainly in my services, acknowledging the many ways that people grieve, honor the dead, and ritualize the hard transition of loss. Yet, even now, I am surprised when folks come up to me after the memorial service and say, "You actually talked about the person who died! That was amazing!

That is when I realized that I am now bi-cultural. Besides being raised in the sensual culture of my youth, I am also now part of a very different culture, which stresses the truthful and loving story of the individual before any particular theology of the mystery of life and death. The Unitarian Universalist memorials that I know stress the life of the person who died. Other religious cultures stress the universality of mortality, and do not lift up the individual. Often the person is just named, and the stories belong to the informal market-square culture of wake, or viewing, or *shiva*, or memorial supper.

Despite the boundaries of religion and culture, personal grieving is not constrained by force of culture or religious or secularized language.

At Devere's memorial, as I spoke, I turned to look at the faces of the people circling around me, and I saw Devere's beloved grandmother, whom I recognized from photographs. I finally would meet her, though after he died. That is when my throat caught, when the visceral grief hit me like a brick, and I had to stop to catch my voice again. It wasn't the religious culture, either of that community or my own, that grabbed my heart. It was his grandmother's face.

I suppose that is true in any culture or religious community or secular group. The complex ritual may be beautiful, or the simplicity of an honest eulogy compelling, but more often, it's one griever meeting another griever that hammers it home.

grief

and relationships

I was talking to my friend Tom recently about a sudden surprise in his life. He told of me of a friendship that had ended ten years earlier. This had been a close friendship, and when it ended, Tom grieved. He understood his part in the break and felt regret and sadness about that, but he also realized that there was nothing he could do to magically restore the friendship. His friend requested no more communication. Period.

Tom went through all the ragged chapters of grief. The guilt. The anger and the sorrow. The self-questioning. It took a long time for him to make some peace in his own heart about what happened between the two of them. Tom maturely tried to honor his friend's decision by not attempting to make contact with her.

Then, ten years later, the friend contacted him, as if nothing had happened. The sense of communication completely restored to former levels, easy and warm.

Tom told me he simply returned to that friendship. He had grieved and never expected to see or hear from this person again. That is hard work, and he did it so that he could get on with his life. Now his friend is back. And all that grief work is behind him. Their friendship is restored.

This kind of grief is not about death, but the grief work associated with it resembles grief after a death.

I once was teaching a class on the New Testament, and when talking about the Gospel of John, I opined that in the story Lazarus undoubtedly died again. The text says that Jesus raised him from the dead. The story portrays his sisters wailing in grief. But then Lazarus comes back to life and everyone rejoices. But nowhere does it say he was raised to life forever. Presumably, Mary and Martha, if they survived him that second time too, had to start the grieving process all over again, when Lazarus got sick and died again.

This notion of grieving *twice* provoked quite a conversation! We all had stories in which we had grieved a loss, usually the loss of a friendship, and then the person in question suddenly showed back up in our lives, changed and tender.

I had an experience similar to Tom's. I lost a dear friend with whom I had spent at least one day a week for many, many years. Long, deep conversations, late dinners, the real affection of touch, laughter, tears; a full, rounded friendship that makes life worthwhile.

One day it was over. Unlike Tom, I really wasn't sure why, exactly. He called, told me his mother had received a cancer diagnosis, and said, "You work with this sort of thing all the time in your ministry, and I have no idea how to respond to such news." We talked together for some time—about his feelings, about his mother—and then at the end, out of the blue, with no indication that anything I had done had sparked this, he said this amazing sentence: "Another thing. I don't think I want to be your friend anymore."

If he had slugged me with a baseball bat, it would have been less painful. I asked, "What? Why?"

He just restated that our friendship was over. We had had a few tensions over the years, but nothing that predicted serious, unresolvable issues. Our friendship always seemed to glow, as far as I was concerned. And we had just talked about something only friends would talk about. But he offered no reason, saying only, "It's not anything you did."

That phone call was the first time I understood what the words *crazy making* meant. I had no indication what was going on with him. Zip. I felt confused, bewildered, and dizzy. He cut off all communication. He wouldn't speak to me if I walked past him on the street. He acted as if I didn't exist.

He was clearly going through something in his beautiful heart I didn't understand. I was angry; oh, was I angry! But eventually I had to give in and say to my soul, "I don't understand and cannot find a way *to* understand, and now I have to live with this strange loss all of my days." For years we lived near each other, but our hearts were far apart. I went through all the chapters of grief I knew from experiencing friends dying. And the chapters were dense, hot, jagged, since the situation was so strange, so unfinished, so like a death, yet not a death.

Then one day, about four years later, he called to say he was sorry. I didn't even recognize his voice when I picked up the phone. He knew how hurt I was, he told me, but he wanted to reach out. As soon as I realized it was him, I wept. Tears erupted, hot and copious. It felt like some miracle, since my grief work, especially the anger, had pretty much removed him from the place in my heart where he had once dwelled.

Our phone conversation was tentative through my tears. I wasn't sure I even believed it was happening. I thanked him for calling (profusely, I have to say), since I no longer felt crazy, and we agreed to meet. When we did, we walked and talked, and I began to understand. He and I talked about my friend Stephen, who was once his roommate, and whose memorial he missed. I told him how that upset me. He revealed the twists and turns in his own heart. I let him see my brokenness, my tears.

We reached out to each other again, cautiously, but our hearts did stretch far that day.

When I moved, he visited me in Columbus, and I visited him back in California. I just got off the phone with him now, and these days our hearts flow easily, as they used to. Neither of us feels confused anymore. We are friends again. I love him tenderly.

Was all that grief wasted? Unnecessary?

Not at all. I am slowly learning that I may have to grieve more than once for many people. Grief can be like a tide, flowing in and flowing out, depending on circumstances, each of which, I've come to believe, is unique to each person.

In fact, when friends of mine have been dying over a long period, always at some point I have begun my grieving before they died. Anticipatory grief. Imagining now life without them, especially when they are in terrible health. Then they rally, and I set that preparatory process on a shelf in my soul until the next crisis. Tide in, tide out.

The breakup of romantic relationships or marriages or partnerships can sometimes add another chapter to the book of grief. I see often in my ministry that people who are separating express not only anger but also bewilderment, sorrow, bargaining, and all the rest, but they also live with a too-often-unexpressed shame. They tell themselves it wasn't *supposed* to be this way. Their grandparents were married for sixty-four years, their parents are still married after forty-five. They tell themselves not that they have failed but that they *are* failures, a rather terrible self-indictment.

Sometimes same-gender couples feel even deeper shame. "We knew it!" they may imagine people saying. "We knew it. We knew folks like you had no capacity for commitment." Shame, on top of all the other emotions associated with grief, can be like a jolt of curare, paralyzing you, preventing you from fully feeling anything else.

I went through some of this shame myself when my partnership broke up. The tears were there, but at times I couldn't weep, because the sense of shame was more powerful. As I worked through the shame, other aspects of my grief flowed more freely, and I was able to move forward.

Grief for losses of all kinds eventually crosses every path we walk. Buddha's 2,400-year-old insight has not dimmed, it seems. Recognizing that, meditating on that reality every day, is something I have come to do in my later years. This does not mean that I do not love deeply, but I set my love in the context of what Buddhists call the Second Noble Truth, which is that the source of suffering (*dukkha*) on earth comes from craving permanence, from imagining that loss is somehow avoidable or that one can be the great exception to the random distribution of suffering around the earth. None of us can be. More and more, I try to see both my love and my grief as aspects of the flow and becoming of my life.

I was not always this way, but as I mentioned earlier, aging is a kind of "compulsory Buddhism."

Tom's story has opened up a whole new perspective on grief for me, and for this I am especially grateful.

grief

and dance

Living in the Oakland/San Francisco area during the eighties and early nineties was a master class in grief. Not only were people I knew and often loved dying almost every week from HIV, but the dead were blamed for their own deaths, and cursed by voices on the political and religious right.

Family members feared hugging their own children for fear of contagion, given the widespread ignorance at the time about the medical aspects of HIV. When officials announced that HIV could be detected in human saliva, the panic about kissing paralyzed us all, and intimacy waned.

One man responded to this panic boldly—Keith Hennessy. One night I attended a performance art piece choreographed and performed by him in the alleys of

San Francisco. It took place under a canopy of sorts, in which two freeway viaducts came together to form both a roof and, toward the back, between two supporting columns, a sort of proscenium.

The piece, stunningly enough, was called *Saliva*. It was in three acts, each performed closer and closer to the actual "stage" under the freeway. The last movement involved torches, a crystal chalice, and choreography calling to my mind the etchings of William Blake (especially "The Dance of Albion"). Keith loudly recited an incandescent poem as he danced, speaking of God, life, and death, and embodying the spirit as he moved, powerfully. I wept at the end. I thought of the story of John the Baptist in the wilderness, crying out for justice. Keith was like that. I felt that the grief saturating my being was being met by a power equal to it, and this helped me to embrace my life as it was. It was my first realization of the power of dance to address grief and to situate it more fully in my life. Panic subsided. Hope leapt, like Keith.

I should have known that the two were connected. In those days, I used to go out often with friends to dance at various clubs. My inner life found shelter in those loud and dazzling rooms, and I often reflected on the lives of friends who had died. Sometimes I would weep as I danced. I was moving around in a crowd, but felt kissed by a sacred solitude in the midst of it.

But the deepest revelation was the night I attended the Bill T. Jones dance *Still/Here* at Zellerbach Auditorium in

Berkeley. Earlier that day we had all gathered at Colma Cemetery to bury Stephen. It had been a draining day, but I had been a Bill T. Jones/Arnie Zane Dance Company guy since the first time I saw them. I decided I needed a blessing of power and beauty at the end of that day.

I got what I wanted and more. It was a multimedia performance—dance and music, but also videos, elaborate colored lighting, and a simple, but monumental architectural set.

Still/Here was created mindful of the impact of younger deaths due to AIDS and prostate and breast cancer. I was so touched by the performance I could not get up at the intermission. I needed to stay in the great theater, soaking in the sensations that were working through my body.

At the end of the second act, Bill, as he always did, invited folks who wanted to stay a bit later to come closer to the stage and have a conversation with him and with all the dancers. I had always attended these sessions, but had never said a word; listening to Bill speak with his entirely reliable depth and elegance was always enough for me.

This time, however, I spoke. I said, "I have both a question and a statement. The question is this: The color lighting during the performance reminded me several times of the rich blues and purples of Monet's water lily paintings. Was that deliberate, or was I reading something into that?"

He smiled and said, "Those are my favorite paintings. I worked with the lighting director, certainly, and I did not mention those paintings, but I wonder if my love for those pieces entered into our conversations about color. Interesting that you noticed that."

"Thank you," I said. "Now here is my statement. I want you to know what you did for me this evening. Before coming here, I said Kaddish as I buried my best friend this morning."

"I said Kaddish when I buried Arne. I know the prayer well. I'm sorry for your loss."

"Thank you. So, here's what I experienced tonight. I felt that in tonight's performance, you put out your hand, and offered it to me. I took it, and you led me up to a high mountain. When we got there, there were tens of thousands of people. You bid us all join hands. They were all people who were grieving like me. All people who had lost someone they loved. Then you stretched out your hand and pointed to all the people there below, the billions of human beings moving about the earth. And you said, 'All of these will be as you are, sooner or later.' Then it felt as if you bid us squeeze each other's hands. I felt as if I was part of a saving community. I can't thank you enough for taking me there."

"Thank you for saying that: it's what I intended in this choreography. But did you feel manipulated?"

At first the question confused me, and then I remembered that a reviewer in the *New Yorker* had written a piece that I felt was both insulting and hurtful about *Still/Here* (and that was just *my* reaction; I can't imagine how it tore up Mr. Jones). So I said, "No, I hope I said to you that you *extended* your hand to me, to all of us. You didn't *take* our hand, you *offered* yours. I was not manipulated at all. It was a gift to my grief that you offered to me. You made me realize I was part of the largest community on earth, the community of grievers."

Later, after the questions and answers ended, I approached him, wanting to be closer to this man who had illuminated my grief with his art. And he did something he didn't have to do. He noticed me as I approached, and called me up on stage, where he was still talking with people, including his sister. And he came over to me, and not only gave me a hug but held me with a gentle rocking, an affirmation of my state, a comfort, and a mutual recognition.

That a choreographed dance could provide me with such a powerful transformation seems obvious now. My grief is *in my body*; dancers are in their bodies. Dance de-intellectualizes grief, stops me from adding up the "stages of grief" on some grid and fitting myself into it.

There are probably other embodied ways of dealing with grief as well. A friend who is a masseur told me that deep tissue massage often lifts tears out of a person, often surprising them, or even making them feel embarrassed. But afterward, the person receiving the massage can always associate the tears with some particular grief. Even far less physical forms of art can nevertheless shake my body. I know that the first time I saw Picasso's *Guernica*, a black and white painting with a portrait of a grieving mother, a cubist Pieta, my tears splashed my cheeks within minutes. I could feel my own grief flowing with anguish through my body. All because of highly stylized gray abstracted lines in a painting. My own body bent in accumulated grief, an unexpected dance.

Even those who do not relate to modern dance, as I always have, are probably aware that grief itself is a kind of artistic movement of our bodies over time— sometimes bent in weeping; or prone, still in bed, depressed; or leaping high into the air of joy and gratitude; or crouching so that we can better rise up back into our lives. Grief, I think, *is* a dance, which we ourselves choreograph based on our family styles, emotional character, or the social cues given to us as we grew up. A necessary, demanding, and sometimes—from the perspective of our mortality, knowing that nothing ever stays the same—a strangely beautiful dance.

postlude

The Cure

We think we get over things.
We don't get over things.
Or say, we get over the measles
But not a broken heart.
We need to make that distinction.
The things that become a part of our experience
Never become less a part of our experience.
How can I say it?
The way to get over a life is to die.
Short of that, you move with it.
Let the pain be the pain
not in the hope that it will vanish
But in the faith that it will fit in.
And be then not any less pain but true to form.
Because anything natural has an
inherent shape and will flow towards it.
And a life is as natural as a leaf.

That's what we're looking for:
not the end of a thing
but the shape of it.

—Albert Huffstickler

The poet speaks of a broken heart, and that too calls forth all the grief experiences I have outlined. Anger, sorrow, depression, relief, even gratitude. I certainly have experienced a broken heart several times in my long life. And each time, grief brought me back to myself, grief made my soul alive again.

The grief the poet addresses reminds me of something about *all* forms of grief: We incorporate the experiences of grief into our lives—"the shape of" grief and loss, as he puts it—which then brings shape to who we are. Reflecting on our grief can help us understand who we are, why we are the way we are, and in some ways it offers us glimpses of hope by outlining what we are becoming.

Thus, grief can be seen finally as a gift that blesses and illumines our mortality and our very existence in this world, which the human race is depleting every day, never once grieving the loss of species, of whole ecologies, of cultures that perish when the last word of a language that we have never heard of dies on the lips of the old woman who is the last of its speakers.

Psychotherapist Francis Weller's remarkable words from his essay "Drinking the Tears of the World:

Grief as Deep Activism" say all this so powerfully, so beautifully. Since I first read them on his website WisdomBridge, they have given me deep comfort and assurance:

Coming home to grief is sacred work, a powerful practice that confirms what the indigenous soul knows, and what spiritual traditions teach: we are connected to one another. Our fates are bound together. . . . Grief registers the many ways this depth of kinship is assaulted daily. Grief becomes a core element in any peacemaking practice, as it is a central means whereby compassion is quickened, our mutual suffering is acknowledged. . . .

The gift of grief is an affirmation of life, and of our intimacy with the world. It is risky to stay vulnerable in a culture dedicated to death, but without our willingness to stand witness through the power of our grief, we will not be able to stem the hemorrhaging of our communities, the senseless destruction of ecologies or the basic tyranny of monotonous existence. Each of these moves pushes us closer to the edge of the wasteland, a place where malls and cyberspace become our daily bread and our sensual lives diminish. Grief instead, stirs the heart, is indeed the song of a soul alive.

Weller's brilliant affirmation provides the conclusion of my book on grief. May it affirm your life as it has my own.

Love, be with us in all our beginnings and endings.

about the author

Rev. Dr. Mark Belletini, a Detroiter, is in his final year in ministry, after thirty-seven years serving Unitarian Universalist congregations in San Francisco and Hayward, California, and in Columbus, Ohio, which is now his home. He served for six years as the chair of the UUA Hymnbook Resources Commission, which created *Singing the Living Tradition*, a hymnbook for use in progressive religious congregations. He was awarded a *Divinitatis Doctor* from Meadville Lombard in 1994 and has taught courses at Starr King School for the Ministry and Meadville Lombard Theological School. He is a visual artist and poet, and spending quality time with his friends, and especially with his son, Tony, grounds his life in love. He is the author of *Sonata for Voice and Silence*, the 2008 UUA meditation manual published by Skinner House Books and available from the UUA Bookstore: **www.uuabookstore.org.**